A Dieter's Companion

*To amuse while you lose
and entertain when you gain*

By
Jeff Howard
(Culinarian and Poet at "extra" large)

In association with
Mr. Riley Octavius Beece

Acknowledgements

Book Cover Art:

[sangoiri] © 123RF.com.
[Elnur Amikishiyev] © 123RF.com.
[Stock Photo] © 123RF.com.

Unmentionable Cuisine
by Calvin W. Schwabe

Special thanks to Cindy for
Book Cover Design and Manuscript Formatting:
www.fiverr.com/graficmonster

Author's Email:
jeffhoward451@gmail.com

CONDOLENCES!

To all my fellow fatties struggling with your weight Condolences! I feel you my lap band of brothers (and sisters of the plus size pantsuit). Fat is like the tar baby in the famed Uncle Remus story, we can move it around but can't seem to get away from it.

My qualifications for commiserating with you on living fat challenged in the modern world is simple. I have been "fat" all my life. A relative term, I would love to be at my college "fat" again but alas I'm far from it. Mother insisted my weight spiraled out of control after I left the nest. When my sister reminded her that she sent me to Weight Watchers in the eighth grade, she had no reply.

Yes the eighth grade my first diet, my first failed attempt but SO not my last. The embarrassment of that first meeting. A fore shadow of diets to come. The adults in the room were all a twitter about how "a cup" of air popped popcorn was such a great snack! So much food! The room broke into laughter when a chubby eighth grader trying his best to be serious asked a one word question.

"Un-popped?" So began my life long journey to morbid obesity.

I am a Chef, the worst of our tribe (or best depending on your point of view). I am a caloric Mephistopheles, the Pied Piper of and for the pudgy, your carbohydrate pusher man. I am very good at what I do, all Chefs(even the terrible ones) say that but trust me I am. My life has been spent in fine dining restaurants, four star hotels and country clubs catering to the one percent. I am surrounded by the finest food their money can buy; Belgium chocolate, heavy cream, slow churned butter, pure maple syrup, prime quality beef, truffle oil and so much more. All my favorite food groups!

I presently spend most of my culinary day in the pastry kitchen. A carbohydrate lover in the pastry kitchen, it doesn't get much better than that. I have five varieties of chocolate within reach, and believe me I've reached.

I so know what you are thinking, culinary work was not a smart choice for a fat challenged individual such as myself but as I told one of my Sous Chefs when he came into my office pouting because the doctor who performed his shoulder surgery called him stupid. (The doc told him not to baby his shoulder after surgery so he went out surfing.)

"Yes! We chefs are tough but we're not too smart!"

It didn't sooth his mood but I thought it was funny. It seems I was born with the kitchen in my blood. In highschool it was custom to exchange yearbooks with each other to write personal notes on the inner covers to be read later in life. My friends wrote comments like "great bread!" and "nice pie!". I don't remember making the bread or pie now that I am in my older years (marijuana taking its toll most likely) but I was a culinarian even back then. Some things just can't be explained logically. It was in my stars to be a chef.

I love the earthy, ribald, creative and politically incorrect environment called a kitchen. Going on forty years my career close to its end and I still wish I could do it all again. Unique personalities are found in kitchens from all corners of the globe. And the partying? THAT was a perk that my youthful self really enjoyed! Never a dull moment I miss the drugs of my youth. I would fall asleep working nine to five at a desk.

Culinary work takes its toll. Each time I changed jobs (which happens frequently in a culinary career) I'd gain twenty pounds. Eating to test, eating from stress, picking all day at work and at play. Living life in the culinary fast lane leads to a plus sized existence in life's fat lane as my eating habits generalized to supersize when "a bite" of cheesecake became a slice! During one weight loss attempt I wrote down everything I picked at during the day. It totaled just shy of three thousand calories, the picking not the meals. Small wonder I packed on the pounds. My weight peaked five pounds shy of four hundred, my fellow fatties can empathize with that fluffy hell.

While overweight chefs are somewhat understandable, what about the rest of society? Sixty percent of people in the U.S.A. are overweight with approximately thirty percent morbidly obese. There are fat accountants, obese politicians, corpulent corporate guys and more to love mommies all around, what's up? Face it my fellow members of the tribe of the "big boned" we have arrived at a time and place, both geographically and historically, where finding food isn't the problem, resisting it is. Food is ubiquitous, the battle against caloric privation has been won. After a lifetime of dieting failures and beating myself up for lack of willpower. After feeling stupid on way more than one occasion as the newest miracle cure the Diet Industrial Complex was selling failed to produce a thinner me. I came to the realization that dieting is the aberration. Eating comes naturally to me, it is dieting that takes all my willpower.

The emotional roller-coaster of weight loss and gain seems to have come out of me in the form of poetry. My book is sort of a fatman's manifesto on living fat challenged in the modern world. They (the poems) came out of me faster than a bulimics food after a banquet once I began writing, I guess had a lot of pent up emotions to vent. My emotions (unlike my phenomenal ability to eat) seem to have been suppressed! Why poems? How the heck should I know I am a Chef not a Psychologist! If my cooks found out the teasing will be relentless, kitchens are way too macho for poetry. All I know is the muse came a calling and the poems just started popping out of my drug addled, porous hippy mind for months.

Poems are the literary equivalent of a painter's portrait, words "painting" and capturing an emotional moment in time. The two things that top my "emotional about" list are food and fat. The pleasurable "yin" of eating and the terrible "yang" of weight gain. My book has two sections; The first my poetic musings on being a fatty in modern America culminating with a short essay on my "Hunger Rules" and how they have helped me in my weight loss battle. The second features eclectic poetry on life, love, loss, dogs and hurricanes because hey we fatties have lives too! I hope the poems entertain (if you gain) amuse (when you lose) and hopefully enlighten so you'll lighten!

Maybe you'll have a "Hey that's what I do!" epiphany! A sous chef with whom I once worked said he had the epiphany he was going to be a chef while cleaning out a huge steam jacketed stock pot! If you can have one there you can have one anywhere. I definitely hope there are a few O.M.G. he didn't say that, moments for I am a Chef and we are definitely an earthy bunch! As we like to say in the kitchen; You play with raw meat all day and see how you talk. I leave you with a quote from Fernand Point the great French restaurateur;

"Before judging a thin man, one must get some information. Perhaps he was once fat!" Fat or thin, diet or binge, have fun and try not to beat yourself up! I hope you enjoy the book!

Table of Contents

Chapter One
Living Large

Nostalgic for Apocalypse.....................................11
Living Large..12
Jack Sprat (The Untold Story).............................12
The Mad Fatties Rap..13
Ode to Thigh Fat 15
Self-Realization..15
My Beach Ball..16
Fantasia Hippo Happy..17
Ode du Swine..18
The Coin...19
Horror Scale..19
The Reaper Grins..20
Oh Fat How I love Thee......................................20
Going Rogue..21

Chapter Two
Mind Over Fatter

Eating "A to Z"..23
My Diet..25
Fasting...26
Revolution...26
The Diet is Now..26
The Diet Twilight Zone..27
The Battle of the Binge.......................................28

Eating Speedy I..29
Eating Speedy II...29
Down Size the Supersize..29
Passive Aggression...30
Roundabout...31
Chipping Away I...32
Chipping Away II..32
Hungry is a Blessing...33
How to Lose Blues..33
Late Night Knucklehead Blues....................................34

Chapter Three
Maladies and Miracle Cures

Apnea oh Apnea...36
Fat Hang Ups...37
Do or Die(t)...38
The Plateau..39
Losing the Debate...40
The Insulin Express...40
I Need a Snack!..41
Mid Life Crisis Blues...42
My "Secret" Happy New Year!....................................42
Heart Song..43
Thank You Big Pharma..43
Tea Apology...44
Red Wine for Health!...45

Chapter Four
Fat and Happy?

The Distant Floor...48
Fat Nowhere Man..49
The Land beyond Thin....................................50
Requiem for Sara.. 56
Slimmericks...58
Heavy Haikus..59
Riley Octavius Beece Thinking......................60
Hunger Rules...67
and Remember...93
Ponderously Pondering Silly Fats.................96

Poems Along the Way

Chapter five
Puppies, Canes and Window Panes

New Puppy Walk..104
A Walking Rhyme..104
Three Cheers for Evolution.........................105
Doggy Dreamland..105
Teddy Bear Love...106
Frankenpup...108
A Dogs Tale...109
A Tall Florida Tale...115
Hurricane Wilma..118
A Florida Window..119
My Favorite Window......................................121
My Father's Window.......................................123

Chapter Six
Leftovers

The Jelly Bean Tree...126
A Chef's Christmas..127
Unlikely Angel...129
Mona Lisa...129
Reflection..130
Green Bug... 130
Island Woman...130
Regrets..131
Velvet Knife...131
Alone is.. 132
Poems Dancing...133
The Night Before Election (2004)............................133
Flicker...134
Poor Penny (lotto bling!)...135
Old Folks Moan..136
The Chef's Special..136

Chapter 1
Living Large

Nostalgic for Apocalypse

Imagine yourself back in a time
when your next meal was harder find.
Back when all effort was centered around
hunting and gathering, not going to town.
Back when we didn't get three squares a day.
Back before dinner was a phone call away.
Back when we fatties were the ones that survived
on our stored fat when famine arrived.

Imagine yourself back in a time
before cold storage and night's out to dine.
Back before eating was convenient and nice.
Back before seasoning, sugar and spice.
We ate due to hunger and hunger alone.
We ate roots and berries, we tore flesh from bone.
Back when only the strongest survived.
We fatties kept living, the thin people died!

Now that advantage has turned to a curse.
We the fat challenged are first in the hearse.
Now the skinnys think they're all that
looking down on us because we are fat.
So my dear fatties, in these modern times
remember we're fat because we survived.
Fight that depression my fat challenged friend.
We're an apocalypse away from ruling again!

Living Large

My belly's shrunk a thousand times
then grows back larger, round and fine.
My belly's turned a thousand heads
wondering about the life I've led.
My belly's launched a thousand ships.
For when immersed the tide will shift.
My belly's so immense in size
painted orange it lights the skies.
The calories I need to satiate
are enough to fill a tectonic plate!
My brain says "no" throughout the day
but my belly gets its hormonal way.
In the living large debate
I know which side my stomach takes.

Jack Sprat (The untold story)

We all know the nursery rhyme
of Jack Sprat and his wife
a minor poetic ditty
about their eating life.

"Jack Sprat could eat no fat
His wife could eat no lean.
Together, they (she and Jack)
Would lick the platter clean!"

But dear soul there's more to tell
of Jackie and his wife
the thing that got between them
to end their married life.

For Jack Sprat, he liked her fat
but wifey wanted lean
sticking to a diet
she realized her dream.

But a dream for one is not for all
as his wife was thinning away
The marriage lost when Jackie ran off
with a cute little fatty named Fae!

The Mad Fatties Rap

I'm going on a culinary walk-about!
Looking for the foods that I did without.
Screw being healthy, screw being good
I'm eating all the food in the neighborhood!
Just back up on away from me now that I am eating
or I'll give "finger sandwich" a whole new meaning!
Don't give me that look! Get away from my food!
This diets got me grumpy
don't you screw with my mood!
You say you are a Doctor, some kind of P.H.D.
so how come all the shit you do, never works for me?
Keep your pills and powders, your shots that metabolize
just like a fallen preacher,
your truths have changed to lies.
I don't need your hormones, no endorphins here
I'll expand my personal horizons with pizza and a beer.
Back on up away from me you diet guru phony
unless you got something with cheese and pepperoni!
YOUR PILLS DON'T WORK!
I don't believe what you say

you'll be seeing less of me, I'm walking away.
I'll manage my emotions with a couple beers
and when I get my buzz on don't let me catch you here!
I'm a mad fatty rapping, about my food addiction
and the diet guru parasites exploiting my affliction.
There is no magic bullet, it's all a waste of time
my wallet loses faster than my belly or behind.
That's all I got to say, I'm just here to represent
To tell my fellow fatties save your money for your rent.
Don't fall for infomercials, not a single word
big Pharma wants your money
they don't care about a cure.
Don't listen to the movie stars raking in the dough
like private chef's and trainers
are for average Joes!
Peace! Exploiters! I got something you can kiss!
I get back on diet after I am over being pissed!!!

Ode to Thigh Fat

The fat that dwells between my thighs
isn't meant for human eyes.
Maybe a hippo would stop and stare
at the abundance I've gathered there.
Maybe its passion would arise
gazing on my fatty thighs.

I wonder if a pig would see
my fatty thighs attractively?
Would he look with loving eyes?
Adoring my bouncy, fatty thighs?
Would his piggy heart turn amorous?
Thinking on my thighs so glamorous?
Of course my musing's bottom line
and what I dearly hope to find
living somewhere in this land
a HUMAN female that understands
the glory of these porcine sides
my dimpled...fatty...hairy thighs!

Self Realization

After riding out Hurricane Frances
I saw a news report on how zoo animals
reacted to the passing storm.
The Panthers paced.
The antelope herded together.
The apes hid and
The elephants ate nervously all night long.
It was then I realized...
I, AM A MEMBER OF THE ELEPHANT CLAN

My Beach Ball

Let me tell you about my beach ball,
I take it far and wide
I must really like it
it's impossible to hide.
People always stare at me
walking down the street
a grown man with a beach ball
nowhere near a beach.
I sort of understand
the thoughts behind their eyes
this beach ball that I carry
sure is super-sized!
It makes me walk so funny
I can never see my toes
you would think I hate it
but where I am it goes.
I take it to the beach.
To the warm and sandy shores.
I take it to fine restaurants
barely fitting through the doors.
And I will tell you something
that will surely make you laugh.
There's barely room for water
when I take it to my bath!
I've have tried to end it
my beach ball love affair.
I swear the damn thing's magical
reappearing everywhere.
I'd swear it was a Yo-Yo
though it's big and round.
Every time I lose it

it keeps coming back around.
It isn't multi colored
no red and green or blue.
It's really sort of flesh toned
and kind of hairy to.
If it gets any bigger
I'll be so fat and round
I won't need to walk
I'll just roll about the town!

Fantasia Hippo Happy

Down the stairs I go!
Feeling tight, feather light!
Fantasia-Hippo-ballerina-graceful
I do gravity, it doesn't do me
inertias slave no longer
I'm Free!

Sixty pounds less, feeling blessed.
A hundred to go, coming off slow.
Double stair stepping, future feeling
no fear kneeling! A happy human being!
Can't wait for what's next!
Maybe...Sex?
(with a partner I mean!)

Ode du swine

In praise of pork, my ode du swine
I'm piggy dreaming all the time
from the trotters to the chine
brother pig you're so divine!

Pork I say, the best of meats
the kind believers refuse to eat!
A happy serendipity
none for them and more for me!

I like it stewed, grilled up and fried.
I like it baked; boned, rolled and tied.
I love it smoked and braised in ale,
head cheese with snout, pea soup with tail.

A pig roast with adobo spice.
Korean kalbi served up with rice.
Ribs on grill, and bacon fried.
Crisp chicharones from the hide.

I love you pig, oh brother swine
breakfast, lunch and dinner time!
I can't stop eating and that is why
I've acquired your B.M.I.!

The Coin

On the floor tempting me
metallic U.S. currency.
Glimmering tender of our nation
a cost v. gain valuation.
Will bending down cost me more
than the coinage on the floor?
I look around for help out there
perhaps a table, shelf or chair.
But if there isn't one around
the shiny coin stays
on the ground.

Horror Scale

On the day I couldn't weigh
the world seemed to fall away
time stood still, sound turned grey
on that despairing, dreadful day.
The nurse that weighed me, over nice
embarrassed for me, weighed me twice!
My face was burning, my back was ice
my stomach gripped inside a vice
I felt so sick "too fat" for scale
humiliated beyond the pale.
A life turned into horror tale.
I went in human...
and came out whale.

**(It was back in the day when
doctor scales only went up to 350!)**

The Reaper Grins

I've been told the Reapers grim
darkly clad and rail thin.
But I think the Reaper grins
as we grow our double chins
watching us as we grow fat
the Reaper knows where it's at.

Oh Fat how I Love Thee

Fat! How I love thee
let me count the ways.
I need a break from my T.V.
so I give to you my day.
I'm a happy couch potato
philosopher and king
protected by your velvet folds
from almost everything.
Because of you, I don't tie shoes
clogs and loafers are all I use.
No planes to take, no need to fly
the bastards charge two seats that's why.
Declared infectious by those who know
no invitations no place to go.
A heart unbroken, can't find a date
I stay at home and meditate!
I thank you fat, it's overdue
I got my cake and ate
the WHOLE... damn...thing too!

Going Rogue

Luxuriating in my lack of will
eating for the thrill.
A glowing, oral, manage au trois
my inner fatty coup d'etat
were there words to describe
the caress as each bite slides
to a stomach jonesing for
a switch from shrubs to carnivore.
A bacon cheeseburger with mayo too
double patties, one won't do!
The first bite, I ate a third!
Angels song I swear I heard.
The second bite O...M...G!
oral, orgasmic luxury!
A pause before I eat the rest
long enough to catch my breath.
Complete surrender hands a blur
my gluttony overwhelms demure.
A cheeseburger.....barely chewed
bacon grease and mayo lubed.
Peristaltically caressed
so my kind of oral sex !

Chapter 2
Mind Over Fatter

Eating "A to Z"

One day I had an epiphany!
I was eating from A to Z!
How did simple become complex?
Baby hunger to adult excess?
I took some notes so I could see
my problems alphabetically!
So here are all the reasons I
eat when hunger isn't why!

Always when they say I can't.
(I hide and eat because of that.)

Bedtime is my final chance
to find a little food romance.

Consuming that of least resistance
chips at hand, salad distant.

Drugs remove my inhibitions
and send my diet into remission.

Exercise it burns the carbs
I deserve that candy bar!

Feeling happy, feeling sad
emotional eating, I got it bad.

Got to finish all the rest
consuming all the evidence.

Ice cream is so cool and creamy
it's my favorite oral binky.

Habit eating, a time or place
for stuffing something in my face.

Just because someone's eating
I doesn't mean they need competing.

Kicking back, I watch T.V.
food commercials enable me.

Late night just me alone
my best friend food is always home.

Mom loves seconds on my plate
which I've eaten as of this date.

Now I've finally surmised
Hunger's thirst in disguise.

Out with friends to paint the town
bar food eating takes the crown.

Placing food where I can see
means less for you and more for me.

Quick I chew and quick I swallow
overeating always follows.

Right after my diet meeting
you'll always find me overeating

Sugar is my pusher man
forget cocaine, I'll take the flan!

The day before I start my diet
guarantees an eating riot!

Unique to me for I'm a Chef
always tasting when under stress.

Victim of a Hurricane?
a crisis pass on diet blame!

When I'm driving in my car
coffee and a candy bar.

X-rated best describes
those smooth and creamy chocolate vibes.

You all know that worn out drill
rebound eating from diet pills.

Zounds! All this talk stirs my desire
to snack a little and then retire.

My Diet

Eat grudgingly.
Choose naturally.
Walk frequently.
Vice sparingly.
Strive happily.
Live hungrily.

Fasting

I'm stronger than serotonin
I'm doper than dopamine
I'm ignoring my endorphins
I'm über-dieting.
I'm disregarding hunger
I'm giving it no time
I'm celebrating human
through supremacy of mind.

Revolution

Revolution against myself
my bad habit commonwealth.
Independence! I declare!
I SHALL NOT BE RETURNING THERE!
In the name of those I love
and with the help of God above.
I pledge myself to fight against
the tyranny called ambivalence!

The Diet is Now

It is the instant between candy and mouth.
It is the distance between fridge and the couch.
It is the eon between eating and full
the infinity it takes for hunger to cool.
It is the number of "no's" in my head
from just after dinner to going to bed.
It is me waking for a 3 A.M. prowl
The bottom line is, diet is now!

The Diet Twilight zone

I can eat forever
nothing fills me up.
If I were down to sugar
I'd eat it by the cup.
My diet is long over
the weight is coming back.
My struggle to get thinner
has fallen off the tracks.
I need to reconfigure
my "all consuming" curse
the dietary habits
That have me in reverse!
I'm talking of compulsion
of eating all I own
My canine knows I've bottomed
I'm eating his milk bones!*
My diets lost momentum
it's lost its gravitas
as I ponder why
while eating Hagen Daaz.
I didn't find it there
or while eating old milk bones
My diet's gone away again
to the diet twilight zone.

(*with salt and Dijon mustard....not bad!)

The Battle of the Binge

A binge is just a breath away
waiting...
Primal craving here to stay
waiting...
It writhes beneath impatiently
it never sleeps
it never rests
it always tests.
It is the primitive
in my soul thriving
from times before
consciousness.
An instinct chained
for a time...
by the mind
until it rises
from behind
my will
my intellect
escaping
through my doubt
battering my self-worth.
Don't let it win
fight it
diet!
The battle of the binge
has begun!

Eating Speedy I

Damn! Slow down the eating speed!
a metronome is what I need
slowing my impressive pace.
The speed at which I stuff my face.
Slow the rhythm, slow the beat
change the habits of how I eat
the only trophy for this race
is the one I wear around my waist!

Eating Speedy II

Eating speedy, eating greedy
How'd we fatties get so needy?
Massive quantities of fast food goo
A diet wasteland is what we do.
Could it be it's our intent?
To find endangered nutrients?

Downsize the Super-size

Downsize the super-size
resist my urge to splurge
searching for a compromise
between my future and an urge.
I need to build an image past uncertainty
of that which I desire that thinner, inner me.
I've got to make a deal
between my cravings and my needs
a renegotiation before fat hangs to my knees!
A reconciliation with my inner child

to realign my cravings from infinite to mild.
Have it my way? On the Highway?
Pass that drive thru by!
O.K., not every day, would every other fly?
I need to tamp the impulse
my warp speed eating gift.
Compromise on portions
and slow it down a bit.
Down size the super-size
resist the urge to splurge
A boy on elephant compromise
where brain and instinct merge!

Passive Aggression

I have a compulsion, fueled by revulsion
that propels my desire to consume.
A powerful potion of pre-cognizant notions
a childhood weapon I groomed.
Passive aggression, my treasured possession
has worn out its welcome of late.
Caloric infusion for parental confusion
has morphed into something I hate.
It's mature version, features dispersion
it's gone rogue, it's stopped being fun.
I say in conclusion, I need a solution
I'm tired of being rotund!

Roundabout

I navigate two roundabouts while I am driving home.
One is for my auto, the other's all my own.
Experience helps me navigate
the one that's on my drive.
The other, purely mental
is redundantly contrived.
I'd have to say it's "same old"
as in "same old tired debate"
between my urge to stop and snack
and hope for losing weight.
A nightly conversation
with excuses trumping doubt
For a dangerous caloric detour
to my "lets binge" roundabout.
A tenacious conversation
percolated by an urge
that creates dynamic tension
where brain and instinct merge.
Passing by my favorites stores
bars and fast food joints
reboots my pesky neural loop to its starting point.
A driver as well as passenger that is how I feel
lost in a mental roundabout
with impulse at the wheel.
The latter won the day this time
the last store while going home.
I stopped for cake and candy
a junk food gastronome.
But dear reader I must say
some willpower was invoked.
I "rounded" out my shopping with a diet coke!

Chipping Away I

Chipping away, chipping away
chipping away my fat.
Trying to uncover
my pre-binge artifact.
It's buried under fifty years
of caloric sediment
it chips away so slowly
I'd swear it was cement!

Chipping Away II

Chipping away my old lifestyle
from party guy to pre-senile.
Retired hippy gone to seed
got too fat from smoking weed.
Chipping away at fifty years
of midnight munchies and drinking beer.
From crypto-bong-hit highs fantastic
to a gut that's turned elastic!
It sure was more fun getting high
than living life, an old fat guy.

Hungry is a blessing

Hungry is a blessing
no more second guessing
in my struggles to avoid
the slightest hungry feeling!
For overeating sets a mood
that starts with guilt and ends in brood.
There's no need to second guess
the choice is hungry or depressed.

(Stay hungry my friends!)

How to lose blues

How hungry can I get?
How hungry can I stay?
How little can I eat
to make it through my day?
How healthy can I choose?
it ain't no pleasure cruise!
Discomfort is the blues
I have to live to lose!

Late Night Knucklehead Blues

Late night on the couch, in a remote clicking slouch
the T.V. and I are up late.
The stooges are on and it doesn't take long
to sink to their comical state.
It's said that we dudes surf for skin on the tube*
but my thing is foodie commercials.
I'm like Pavlov's dog when those things come on
stuck in a habitual circle.
A food ad oh my! To the fridge on the fly!
A food stooge in locomotion!
Old Curly and me, fine stooges are we
brains overruled by emotion!
Larry's there too, he's playing the fool
like me eating all I desire.
But what Moe has just said has stuck in my head
simple, and yet so inspired.
"WAKE UP! GO TO SLEEP!" it's no mental feat!
a stooge cannot eat in mid-slumber
So the comedy that's me, at a quarter to three
retires just slightly rotund-er !!

(*Not to say that I never surf for skin on the tube!)

Chapter 3

Maladies
and Miracle Cures

Apnea oh Apnea

Apnea oh Apnea
you robber of nap-knee-uhs
your tortures are subtle and stealthy.
You do let me sleep
only just not too deep
so I'm between sick and healthy!

I am feeling deprived
between dead and alive
so slowly you're trying to slay me.
In deep sleep when I rest
you block all my breath
and then on the brink, you save me.

I wake up at night
In a cold sweaty fright
my heart is beating like crazy.
I sit there and think
while my hearts on the brink
am I sick or just going crazy?

The beds soaked with sweat
from my struggle for breath
but I'll tell you what's even sadder.
It's simply the worst
another apnea curse
losing control of my bladder!

But now I've come clean
with my C-PAP machine
the benefits of science I'm reaping.
The Docs I adore
and I thank them once more
for returning the dreams to my sleeping!

?
Fat
Hang Ups

?
Fat
hanging
everywhere
getting old ain't no joke
under this heavy fatty yoke
bound to food like a whore to coke.
?
Fat
enables
my impression
like the mirror at the fair
my reflection looking like a pear
my loss is what I've gained down there.
?
Fat
creeping
all of the time
invading, like a vine
intramuscular......intertwined
my grade improves from choice to prime.
?
Fat
ruling
heart and mind
willpower undermined
dictates of a primal kind
whispered urges consume my time.

?
Fat
dashing
every dream
fatty layers muffling
any budding social scene
my best friend food so comforting.
?
Fat
hang Ups
pervade my life
invading all aspects
becoming the cruel midwife
who I must lose to get on with life!
?
Fat
hang ups
hanging me up!
They sure got me thinking
about a life that's shrinking
from a waistline that's expanding!

Do or Die(t)

Me, myself and I
must give a diet a try
or prematurely die
me, myself and I.

The Plateau

I was good all week
and the scale didn't move.
I was good all week
but it says I didn't lose.

DAMN IT!!

I'll just go out and eat,
it doesn't pay to try,
how am I supposed to feel
when the damn thing tells a lie?

I HATE IT BAD!
THAT AWFUL THING!

All knowing, never wrong
the diet god who's judging me
accusing me of wrong.
In its bathroom temple
silently it screams!
NO compassion, no forgiving
that gosh darn thing is mean!
I was good all week
why does it treat me so?

I HATE IT!
I AVOID IT!
I have to get on it.......
I WAS GOOD ALL WEEK!!!!!

Losing the Debate

While driving at night, alone in my car
I engage in debate before going far.
The fact I'm alone doesn't matter too much
my brain and desires are more than enough.
A tired old chat that's always about
staying on diet or just pigging out.
An inner debate that always begins
with weak rationales for starting a binge.
A binge on the make, a sad place to be
as the diet I'm on sinks into a sea
of impulsive eating as I figure out why
the hows and the whys of it going awry.
Depression begins and enables what's next
the binge has begun, I've returned to regressed!
So I abandon the diet for a sugar rush high
and guilt replaces my willpowers sigh.

The Insulin Express

I ride a roller coaster
called "The Insulin Express".
It takes me to the highest high
then drops me to depressed.
Every time I ride it
I swear it is my last
but I always go back on it
the high is such a blast.

I need a snack!

Lost in a sea
Of people smarter than me.
Creating molecules I can't absorb.
Sorbitol disturbs my core.
Serotonin is such a bore.
Insuring me makes them more.
Trainers train elliptically.
Preachers diet biblically.
Doctors speaking critically.
Take this pill!
Drink this swill!
Health's no thrill!
I'm feeling ill!
I got no knees!
D.V.T.s!!
Godly pleas...
Oh God PLEASE!!
Blood sugar high
my oh My!
pulmonary emboli!
Oh my back
HEART ATTACK!
I need some slack.
Life is whack!
no small wonder
I need a snack...

Mid Life Crisis Blues

Another day of mid aged grey
with yet another on the way.
Same old job for the same old pay.
same old, same old, thrills and play.
A romance ends the same old way
as another other fades away.
Same old God up there on high
with different names to justify
the righteousness of who should die
in their wars for the same old lies.
Higher taxes, bills and dues
the same old midlife crisis blues.

My "Secret" Happy New Year!

Health, wealth, and happiness!
I toast the coming year!
When all my dreams will come to pass
and riches will appear!
My dieting will find success
the pounds will melt away
as I live on the healthy side
of each and every day!

Health, wealth, and happiness!
this is the stellar year
when a lifestyle only dreamt of
will miraculously appear!
I'll have success in business
more than I had planned
and live a life of leisure
a happy, wealthy man!

Heart Song

The nagging narrative in my head
is inspiration's watershed.
Admonitions in my mind
pejorative and well defined.
Advocating it appears
the latter choice of hope and fear.
When my mind is stuck on "why?"
imagination will never fly!
Now the little voices, they depart
direct from infinite to my heart.
Wordless whisperings to my soul
from the place where good things flow.
Creative urgings that realize
all things art and all things wise.
So quiet the voices in my head
and listen to my heart instead.

Thank you Big Pharma

Waking happy! Feeling spry!
Welcome back! my oh my!
Laying down but standing tall
my tiny dancer needs a ball!
All week long, feeling blessed
adolescent thought obsessed!
My resurrection didn't last
middle age renewed its grasp.
The sad but true reality
the surge in my vitality
was not a gift from up above.
Big Pharma authored in my love.
Delight diminished upon refill
mistook Viagra for my other pill.

Tea Apology

First of all my apology
to anyone that loves their tea.
To the subjects of Queen and Czar
to those in the east both mid and far
I am sorry folks but I can not see
any reason for drinking tea.

I've tried them all from black to green
and I'm still search FOR CAFFEINE!
It's kissing your sister, need I say more?
I haven't found any I like at the store!
Especially the spiced ones I've given a try
tasting like water and smelling like pie.
Then there are those I wouldn't drink on a bet
like Spiced Serendipity, or Herbal Tibet.
I've added some lemon, I've spiked it with rum
with negative pleasure (except the last one).

I know from the news the Docs think that it's great
it helps to fight cancer, it helps to lose weight.
But even enlightened with these bits of news
drinking that stuff just gives me the blues.
Now COFFEE my friends, is my drink of choice
it turns my MOARNings into rejoice!
So despite the findings this coffee-head says
I'm hanging with my homey
Old Juan Valdez.

Red Wine for Health

It's been around since before the flood
and now they say, it helps my blood?
Good for colon health as well?
Could it really be that swell?
I just read the other day
wine helps to keep some cancers away.

Pondering this miracle drink
I figured a glass would help me think.
I don't feel different, the jury...still out
so I tip another to remove any doubt.
A skeptic, scientist and poet am I
So another glass empty
here's mud in your eye!

Well so far i see no change at all
but I got to admit I'm having a ball.
The more wine I drink, more sense it makes
I got to keeps trying ..for sciences sake!
After, after all I'm de-determined guy
A third glass I raise "Toooo health!" says i!

Damnnn...I am beginning to ce
how kerect the scientists could b.
I feels sooo good, I feesl sooooo fi...fi... finnne
Gonna drink this stuff all da thyme
It sure helps me with my ry...ry...rrrhyme
Gimme na..na…nother glass o' wine!

I convince, dose guys wer right!
Wine makin me feel Tiiiight!!
I shud do this every nite!
Take cair o my health, keep feel fine
Bless that good ol bottle wa..wa..wine
Maybe just maybe...have 2b sure
I open anudder ba...ba….bottle wyne….

Reservatrol for Health?
Drink 100 bottles? Koooolll…..

Editor's Note:
The poet has disappeared and cannot be
Located as of this date.

Chapter 4
Fat and Happy?

The Distant Floor

Now here's a poem of what's in store
for a fatty, and the distant floor.
Thin people just can't relate
to what we fatties contemplate
just before we begin to bend
to facilitate our rise again.
When I bend in my blimp like state
my backbone surely laments its fate.
My eyes bulge out, my forehead aches
I cannot breath, my lungs deflate.
So just before the trip on down
I give a subtle glance around
to make sure that no one sees
a bug-eyed fatty with aching knees.

To get the flavor, let's take a trip
back to my apprenticeship.
A hotel kitchen large and fine
with refrigerators, the walk-in kind.
Once I opened the walk-in door
and saw him floundering on the floor.
Chef François was laid out flat
arms outstretched, and Orca fat.
Desperately he was gathering in
broccoli spilled out from a bin.
His fat red face, it turned to beet
when he saw my clog clad feet.
Relief set in when he looked up
a mere apprentice helped him up.

Back then it was a funny thing
fat François floundering
But now I have more empathy
for now I'm as fat as he!
Let me describe a couple more
barriers between fat and floor.
If no hand hold is nearby
we fatties don't begin to try
and like a hidden closet queen
we do not relish being seen.
So if a handhold isn't found
or if someone is around.
What got dropped stays on the ground.

Fat Nowhere Man

Fat man walking his last mile
short steps only, it takes a while.
Short breaths taken, his color pale
shoulders aching, knee joints wail.
His back protests the hard cement
punishment for a life ill spent.
Fat man walking without grace or smile
"It sucks to be you" is his lifestyle.

Thin people know with nary a doubt
his obvious failings, of what he's about.
"Just stop eating! It's easy to see!"
The fault is in you, thank god it's not me!
No willpower that's it! That must be the thing!
"You're lazy! Defective! A total weakling!"
They could care less where his feelings are at
bigotry's cool for the excessively fat.

A fat man walks down street ridicule
a lonely back alley in a city of cruel.
No one sees past his layers of fat
to find out where the human is at.
A fat Quasimodo he shuffles along
in the periphery which is where he belongs.
In the near future he'll stop being there
and no one will notice
no one will care.

The Land Beyond Thin

Let me tell you the tale of my travels within
a frayed paradise called The Land Beyond Thin!
A paradise surely, all honey and cream
from shore to horizon, a food lover's dream.
I traveled around it for many a year
a journey of pleasure seasoned with tears.
I wish I had known before I began
the cost would be more than originally planned.

In the beginning, I have to confess
this food lovers dream surely impressed.
The Land Beyond Thin was a marvelous place
heaven on earth from the sugar god's grace.
Confections galore lined hard candy paths
that led up to mountains of sweet chocolate hash
each peak had a dollop of French meringue fluff
The Land Beyond Thin, it had the right stuff!

While wandering down its white sugar beaches
eating shells tasting like candy glazed peaches.
While drinking ambrosia from the sweet ocean blue
that could easily double for a great fruit fondue.
While watching waves churn to a chantilly cream
I had an epiphany! A moment's day dream!
A hike to the mountains from the blueberry sea
was just what was needed for the foodie in me!

I spotted a path made of butterscotch candy
all sunny and yellow and looking quite dandy.
The "Yellow Brick Road" for my chocolaty quest
unaware that like Dorothy I'd be facing some tests!
But there at the start there was so much to see
like candy cane lamp posts and pulled sugar trees.
The path ran beside a warm ganache stream
that surely flowed down from my chocolaty dream.
But a path that seemed simple, path that looked straight
produced a surprise and altered my fate.

She appeared out of nowhere all happy and gay
a smoky eyed genie named Sweet Mary J.
Her voice was seductive so sensual and full
she smelled of the forest, of pine trees and dew.
Her skin shade, milk chocolate, her hair caramel
that sexy old genie just rang all my bells!
She snuggled up close and whispered so sweet
"Just tell me big boy and I'll make it complete!"

Pleased and befuddled by that sexy Creole
I expanded my quest to a manlier goal!
"I want to experience every inch of this land!"
"I want to taste EVERYTHING from simple to grand!"
"Are you sure?" she asked suppressing a yawn
then hugged me and kissed me and poof she was gone!
Dazed and hungry, again on my own
I spotted her note on a butterscotch stone.
"Watch out what you wish for." is what it said.
"See more of you later." In script, cherry red.

From that very day food became my best friend
my alpha and omega, my beginning and end.
I became somewhat famous, I was known in the land
when the subject was food, I was always the man!
I worked and I played and packed on the pounds
in cheesecake factories and chocolate towns.
Living the pleasure as my days turned to years
from the finest French food to pizza and beer.
From humble breading pudding to truffles galore
I ate and I ate and I still wanted more!
The thing so amazing, the thing that was cool
I ate and I ate…but I never felt full.

Those years so enjoyable extracted a toll.
My weigh spiraled upwards, out of control.
At the foot of the mountains I decided to rest
debating the wisdom of my chocolaty quest.
I stopped at an Inn, the famed Chanteclaire
To visit my friend, Chef Jean Luc Pierre.
A king among chefs, old Jean was the one
emotional, artistic and extremely rotund.

There at his table in the back of the room
I saw my friend sitting in mutter and fume.
The tension was palpable, it hung in the air
but we met and we hugged like two Frigidaire's.
"Zey told me zue creeate...le grand buffet"
"For zee merde eating peegs we get ere deez days!"
His temper exploded when asking him why.
"ALL YOU CAN EAT EZZ ALL ZAY WEEL BUY!!!"

The buffet was impressive, elaborate and grand
baked brie and baguettes was how it began
Scottish smoked salmon was next on the line
accompanied by caviar, Beluga, most fine.
The entrees, mouthwatering, a tempting array.
From duck a la orange, to French cassoulet.
The soufflé potatoes perfumed with gruyere
dissolved on my tongue as if they were air.
The desserts were "la crème" of the French pastry art
Éclairs and napoleons and rainbow fruit tarts.
Chocolate dipped berries and charlottes with pears
surrounded a croquembouche, the tallest piece there.
Almond puff pastries and a Saint Honoré
were only surpassed by the warm crème Brule.

Over cognac and coffee, I sat calming my friend
hoping he wouldn't get angry again.
But he was too drunk from drinking Pernod
he just erupted! he seemed to explode!
He stood up and launched a profanity steam
turned purple and DIED in mid-blasphemous scream.
I stayed for the funeral bidding old Jean goodbye
then back on the road to ponder life's whys.
The closer I got to that bittersweet hill

the more gluttony it took to give me a thrill.
A body that started in such youthful shape
had morph to a pear before blooming to grape.
While resting beside a crème anglaise pond
under palm trees lined with marzipan fronds.
I realized this was more nightmare than dream
the land beyond thin wasn't peaches and cream.

.

Between me and the mountains I had finally reached
stood a gingerbread castle all broken and breached.
The pilgrims trudged through it too tired to care
of the hows and the whys of such disrepair.
The sign on the gateway; "The Land Beyond Hope
ruled by her highness Queen Mary of Mope."
I was told in her youth she was happy and gay
until a lost love took all that away.
She had gotten so fat she couldn't sit in her chair
but just kept on eating like she didn't' care.
I bid her good day as I passed the queen by
she looked up and waved a despondent goodbye.

When I stopped for a drink from her chocolaty moat
it was cocoa mass bitter, I coughed and I choked.
All I could think of was Jean Luc Pierre
as I gasped and I struggled while fighting for air.
I dropped to the ground like a lumbering beast
tired and aching and nearly deceased.
When I loosen my "fat" pants quadruple X size
it freed up my thinking and I realized
each step of a journey is built on the last
and the life that you live is built on the past.
At the foot of the mountain I had so longed to see
I realized my health was more important to me.

Steamship slowly, I lumbered around
changing my course and heading back down
off of a mountain I once held so dear
and insult to injury that genie appeared.
I said "Look at me Mary! I'm not happy! I'm FAT!"
She smirked and replied "Well...you never wished that"
and then poof, she was gone, never saw her again
so much for a genie I thought was a friend.
As I started back down I was sick with the fact
food would still tempt me all the way back.
So ends the tale of my journey within
a bittersweet kingdom, The Land Beyond Thin.
To all culinary trekkers, I have two things to say
First please remember, you'll leave it someday
and next, most important if you meet on the way....
DON'T TRUST A GENIE
NAMED SWEET MARY J!

Requiem for Sara

A requiem for Sara
I think that was her name.
Featured in the paper,
two days of local fame.
I think of her from time to time
as my years go by
when I pause to think on things
like life and how and why.

Was she predestine
to become what she became?
A tragedy who's end was death
with obesity to blame?
A kind and generous neighbor
the few who knew her say
the ones that didn't seek her
and thought she moved away.

But she had never left them
suffering her fate
breaking her hip, not once, but twice
from being overweight.
I do know the how and when
but still know not the why
the second time she broke it,
she decided not to try.

She settled down upon her couch
and did not rise again
and sat six years in a fetid hell,
loved ones at wits end.
When the authorities finally found her,
morbidly obese
she had sat in her own filth so long
her skin wove into the seat.

They removed her to the hospital
on that putrid throne
through a gaping exit hole
they cut into her home.
During the attempt to save her
she bid this life farewell.
I wonder how her spirit felt
released from mortal hell.
The joy it must have been
at the moment of release
from her tortured mortal plain
to a realm of peace.
Feather light on angel's wings
to heaven she will fly
and maybe when she gets there…
God will tell her why.

Slimmericks

I once knew a fat guy at work
who thought eating was one of life's perks.
He died most rotund
his gravestone was fun,
It said "Finally a diet that works!"

There once was a guy named McLaughlin
who ate ice cream more than too often.
His belt got so tight
it "banana split" him one night.
So they buried him in two separate coffins!

My gut never leaves me alone
I get up and it wants to stay prone.
In wonderment I
keep pondering why
it's acquired a life all its own!

My diet, I've decided to chuck it
eating sugar and cream by the bucket.
I wish orally,
I'd play calorie free.
(But not like the guy from Nantucket)

We fatties we love self-reflection
not for health or inner perfection
strange as it seems
our musings and dreams
are more in a gluttonous direction!

Heavy Haikus

**(five syllables, seven syllables, five syllables
more or less make up your own!)**

An elevator
struggles, upwardly challenged
for I am in it.

An Atkins belch
turkey with salmon and eggs
serendipity.

Impulse forgotten
how did food get in my mouth?
diet Alzheimer's!

Fat man with salad
thin man with a pizza
take-out injustice.

Orange reflection
the mirror declares my guilt
Cheetos addiction.

Frustrated I stare
the vacuum in the corner
won't work on my fat.

Diet Superman
carbohydrate kryptonite
back to fat Clark Kent.

Riley O. Beece Thinking

The longest relationship I have had in my life is with my fat, I hope it doesn't follow me to heaven. I remember dieting when the only guidelines available were the dietician sheets that I got directly from my father, a doctor. I dieted before dieting was cool. I was less that enamored with it eating was SO much more fun! When I found out I could piss off my parents doing it, well that was sauce for the goose. No one knew about "passive aggression" back then but I sure groomed it to a childhood weapon. My poor parents were just trying to do the right thing but a chubby twelve year old doesn't care about the long game in life.

Stealing food and hidden eating were a game to me. There was a freezer in the basement of my parents' house that held Eskimo pies. For the unenlightened an Eskimo Pie is basically a chocolate covered ice cream bar without a stick. I could steal and eat one in its entirety by the time I reached the top of the stairs, three bites and gone without a brain freeze. Mom bought a lock box out of frustration for all the goodies and snacks so I learned how to pick a lock. All that was five decades ago, I started down the road to fat city young in life.

The boffin's track record for obesity cures is dismal but I can't really blame them. The "beast" (my pet name for my hunger) is nobody's bitch. Hunger is the elder God, the primal imperative, the oldest of the old. Hunger is older than sex! Back when single celled organisms reproduced asexually they still were driven to consume. The Beast is powerful indeed. The Beast compels. The Beast (at the risk of repeating myself) is nobody's bitch.

Back in the day, finding food while not becoming food, was the challenge. But not so in the modern world.

Finding food, for most of us is easy, avoiding it is the problem. Our antediluvian instincts, so important to our survival back in the hunting and gathering days have turned from assets to liabilities. The good life we created with the best of intentions in these modern times comes at a price, measured in calories and paid by the pound. There is no conspiracy, we are the victims of our own success as a species. Food is ubiquitous and at our beck and call.

The road to obesity is pleasure being obese is hell. Putting on my socks at four hundred pounds isn't pretty! Diets, diets, diets, I know them well. Call them Legion for they were many. I have been on too many to count, all of them promising the same thing. Lose weight without hunger. What a crock! Hunger was the ONE thing, every diet I tried had in common! It didn't matter what pill I popped, what injection I bent over for or how well I kept a diary of my food intake hunger was omnipresent, it was God, like I said before it is the BEAST!

Hunger so powerful it even controls my perception of time. When I am dieting, hunger turns minutes into hours and hours into eternity as I sit, dwelling on, salivating to and jonesing for my next feed. When that carefully measured and blandly crafted meal arrives it is, like the movie says "gone in sixty seconds." I've read it takes twenty minutes for the brain to tell the body it's full, my brain missed the memo. I'd inhale my meager meal in five minutes and sit for forty or more meditating on the beast as it clawed at me from deep within, wanting more.

Another bummer dieting fact we fatties know all too well. DIETS ARE BORING! Diets are bland, meager "Please Sir may I have some more?" meal events that leave me wanting every time. Diets are boring combinations of lean proteins and vegetables with all the good stuff restricted, no carbs, fat and fun. Oh, and the "drink lots and lots of water" thing? Is that really is it necessary? Keep out of the fridge and have a bathroom nearby at all times! Eating comes naturally for me, it's dieting that takes all my brain power. The diet industry and I are like daters that don't find love sooner or later we part and not in a good way either.

One doctor, after reading the food journal he told me to write (the butter, the brie and the beef tenderloin with béarnaise) chastised me. I couldn't tell if he was upset from a professional perspective or just jealous of the great food I got. I looked at him and asked,

"What do you want me to do go and graze in the fields like a cow?" I took his gloomy expression and silence as a yes and we parted company.

Another compared me to a drug dealer.

"You don't have to eat your food! Cocaine dealers do not use their product!"

A drug dealer, really? I was so mad after that, I decided not to use his. I wrote the poem *Going Rogue* after that disaster of a diet, all about the joy of eating a double bacon cheeseburger with mayo on the drive home. Soooo delicious! It came in a grease speckled brown paper bag with a ton of fresh cut French fries. U.S.A.! U.S.A.! Great fast food! It might not be healthy, but it sure is fun.

I got to give it up to the good old US of A. We live at a time, in a place, surrounded by abundance. The food industry caters to our every whim. A steaming hot pizza is a phone call away and at my door in thirty minutes or less. In walking distance of my condo: A Cuban restaurant, a Italian Restaurant, two walk up pizza joints, a smoothie bar, a Thai restaurant, a Sushi restaurant, a Panera Bread, a Pollo Tropical. a Rotisserie chicken joint (wood fired oven, delicious), a Mickey D's, a KFC, Five Guys Hamburgers, Subway Subs, Jersey Mikes Subs, a Chinese takeout, a Chinese restaurant, a Dunkin' Doughnuts, a breakfast joint, a waffle house, Applebee's, Starbucks, two sports bars and more. All the burgers, wings and garbage fries I could possibly want in walking distance, not that I walk. I didn't even count all the grocery stores, convenience stores and gas stations. Food is everywhere. I don't blame the food industry I admire them!

It wasn't always this good. Historically there was no "three squares a day" guarantee. Food was harvested or caught. It had to be butchered and prepared, there was no cold storage. The food supply could be interrupted by storms and drought. I have a cookbook of regional and historical recipes (real recipes) called *Unmentionable Cuisine*. I found it browsing at a book store and opened it to "Broiled Puppy - Hawaii" I just had to buy it after that! I remember thinking oh boy I could use this for employee meals!

The recipe that sticks in my mind (besides the broiled puppy) is "Locust stew -Early American Pioneer". Yum locust stew! How much hunger does it take to trigger a desire to eat a big hot steaming bowl of that? I think a few meal periods would have to be missed before locust stew looked like dinner. It falls into my "Zoo Food" category. If it's in a zoo I don't cook it and I sure won't eat it.

The old days weren't all bad. Back then explorers got some great tasting stuff directly at the source. Take for example beaver anal glands! They are used even to this very day in some raspberry flavorings (if you don't believe me, google castoreum). Imagine Lewis exclaiming to Clark back the day,

"Hey Clark! Sacagawea was right! This beaver butt

smells like raspberries, it's delicious!"

In the modern era, the majority of us are fat (around sixty five percent). Thirty percent (like me) are morbidly obese AND evolutionarily unprepared for the "weighty" problem we face namely how not to eat in the midst of all the food! Here's a thought, we fatties aren't that aberrant sixty five percent isn't an aberration it's a majority! We do what most everyone does. We see food and eat it we just happened to store it better. As one scientist said in an article I read,

"It is very hard for a human to pass up offered calories." I mean Duh!

Scientists recently isolated an "aberrant" gene modification in rats that causes some calories to be always stored (as fat) rather than be burned for energy. Back during the hunter-gathering times, I think that gene would be considered a blessing rather than aberrant but no use in complaining about that now. We the corpulent tribe of the big boned, have always been suspicious there was something besides our lazy ways and lack of will (that the skinnies keep telling us about ad nauseam) causing our misery. It is nice to be vindicated take that fat-shamers!

I grew up in an upper middle class, post-great depression family. My parents had grown up in hard times and wanted to make darn sure that their children, weren't going to suffer the hunger they did. We ate three squares a day, each and every day with snacks in between. Hunger? I didn't know it. I only knew that the people in China did. Clean your plate my parents would say, people are starving in China.

Later in life, I had a girlfriend from the West Indies. She told me when she was a child there was always a pot of "peas" on the stove, which from her description, was basically a thick version of bean soup. If she was hungry it was there, day after day, week after week, month after month. No eating for pleasure, no pampered variety, just an ever present pot of dried pea porridge. Eating for her was a necessity, not recreation. She could tolerate, easily tolerate, a level of hunger that would have me scouring the shelves for something to eat. If she got hungry and there was no food, she would go to sleep. If I am hungry I can't sleep! Hunger, my frenemy, is always stalking me. I have gotten so bad, I eat in anticipation of hunger, not from it. I am SO it's bitch.

Now that I am older and on the downward slope of career and ambition, the passions of my youth have waned, but sadly I have become the hot mess that is the aggregate of all the compulsive eating behaviors I've acquired over the years. My phenomenal eating speed and my passive aggressive compulsion have generalized from childhood weapon, through young adult hedonism to adult self-immolation. I was "Hangry" before Hangry was even a word. So many caloric kinks, so little time left to correct them all.

I am much better at gaining weight than losing it. I really love to eat. I have been doing it my whole life and I am darn good at it. My compulsion turned me into a great Chef. The food I make is just SO good! I am surrounded in my kitchen by the best quality of just about everything that one can eat. My French style pastry so good it almost has a sexual aspect to the pleasure consuming it gives.

Each year during my career, my weight would oscillate with an increasing upward spiral until I was five pounds shy of four hundred. Morbid obesity is the name. My pleasurable road of caloric consumption ended in a nice little personal hell on earth. Read my I *Once Traveled in the Land Beyond Thin* poem to get the flavor. Something has to change or my destiny will most likely be premature residency in a triple extra-large coffin. I've always wondered how much fat I'd render during the cremation process. My father told me that human fat and pig fat are very similar and I just love pig fat (*Ode du Swine poem*) but I digress. What to do, what to do, what to frigging do? Becoming thinner is easier said than done in my world. I have cycled through most of the diet programs available, ending up back where I started or worse as each successive year arrived.

A few summers back, I tried a Phentermine enhanced protein diet (Say goodbye to sleep and your sex drive with that pill). I lost ninety one pounds, gaining seventy back during the busy season. The next summer I did a self-supervised protein diet. I lost seventy and gained it all back. The following summer as I glumly contemplated another weight lost attempt I had an epiphany. EATING IS OUR NATURAL STATE IT IS THE DIET THAT IS THE ABERATION! My problem had more to do with my inability to co-exist with hunger during the year as opposed to trying to stick to a diet program that didn't fit the reality in which I was living.

Constantly trying to feel "full" while dieting is an oxymoronic exercise. In primal times before food was omnipresent, hunger was frequently forced upon us. I wanted to create a structure imitating this more natural era of human existence. How could this pejorative condition be recreated voluntarily? Instead of suffering and hating hunger, could I seek it out and co-exist with it simulating the conditions back when "three squares a day" wasn't a given?

One of my college professors once used the analogy of

"a boy on an elephant" to describe how the brain works.

The boy represents our intellect, our conscious thought. The elephant is our primitive, the set of instincts that have been with us since creation. Hunger is my elephant and dieting is my boy. Getting that big old stubborn pachyderm to do what I want isn't easy and sooner or later it always does what it wants.

Can the boy train the elephant to ameliorate some of its excesses? An alcoholic can swear off booze, a smoker can quit tobacco but we fatties have to eat, we all have to eat. A regime that isn't woven into the fabric and ebb and flow of my life is doomed to fail. A new relationship with that big old intractable drive called hunger has to be forged. I have to change who I am to change what I am. I have to remember that primal truth. Hunger rules.

Hunger Rules

My poetry begs the question, what have I learned? One thing and one thing only, HUNGER RULES! Despite what the diet industrial complex says, hunger and weight loss are inseparable. I have news my corpulent homies there will not be an abundance of food and we WILL be hungry on whatever program we choose. When the vivacious rail thin dietician bats her pretty baby blues at you and says;

"Don't worry! There will be plenty of food you will never be hungry!"

Smiling her cute diet tech smile she is selling you a bill of fictitious goods. Her idea of plenty is my idea of an appetizer. She could survive for a week on a meal the size of a postage stamp and I need a bit more than that. There is something to be said about a cute young dietician trying to reach her arms around my massive middle with a tape measure but even that isn't worth the all money I have spent on supervised diet programs guaranteeing weight loss without hunger. It reminds me of what one of my country boy line cooks once said.

"I went on a diet but I was still hungry, so I went on another diet!" (Try to say it with a nice country twang.) Then he laughed, he is my kind of guy.

I have counted calories, measured food, compulsively weighed, kept a diary, injected my stomach with hormones and drank diet protein powders until I was farting dust. But invariably life and the kitchen happened and for whatever reason or rational I had at the time I would lose the diet and gain back the weight. Food is my go to solution for almost everything life throws at me. I am stressed (eat!), I am depressed (eat!), I am happy (eat happily!), I am drunk (eat A LOT!). The boffins say goal related behavior (like a diet), succumbs to gratification behavior (like eating for pleasure) as the stress in one's life increases. I must say you are preaching to the choir there my scientific amigos!

Something had to be done to stop my weighty upward spiral, but what? Obviously what I've been doing hasn't worked. A definition of insanity most of us have heard as some point in our lives: *Insanity is doing the same thing over and over and expecting different results.*

THAT is SO me! I have been dietetically insane for over a half century! Let that sink in and marinated for a bit! Fifty years of diet programs with nothing to show for it. Well my stomach has become magnificent but you know what I mean. My dream of becoming a Chip n' Dales dancer is only going to happen on fat Tuesdays no wonder I get depressed!

As I have said before I've come to the conclusion that I

need to "flip" the script. I want to embrace hunger instead of loathing it. I want to seek out and coexist with a level of hunger that would have had the former me running to the fridge for a snack, which quite frankly is not very much hunger. So I made rules that if followed, build an intellectual structure that creates a new relationship between my hunger and me.

The first eight rules deal with the mechanics of staying hungry. The latter six try to address my attitude which has darkened to fatalistic over my many years of being a fatty. While they are not a magic bullet they give me a chance to make the right choice at the crossroads of intellect and instinct. They give me a chance to travel the righteous path of caloric sobriety when all of me wants to skip on down the pleasurable highway of culinary delight. I repeat them daily so they will embed in and percolate to my consciousness when a choice needs to be made. They represent an opportunity to do the right thing at the intersection of human and animal (Hint when the choice needs to be made it's the one you don't "want" to do!) If I do the opposite of what I want to do often enough, I will get to be what I want to be! (Chip n' dale's here I come!)

I am in my third year and have experienced positive changes. My annual weight gain/loss spread has ameliorated to +20 pounds from as much as +70 by changing the type and quantity of food I eat as well as the exercise I do. I wish I could say the rules were the holy grail of weight loss but alas, I am just another plump duck on the pond trying to figuring things out. But I have hope! My first attempts were positive and hopefully an arbiter of future success. To my fellow fat challenged denizens in the tribe of the corpulent good dieting and best of luck. I hope the book entertains and helps on your journey to thin city!

HUNGER RULES!

1. Get, stay, like and do things hungry, as long and as often possible.
2. Prep, plate, sit and eat my meals at a slow and measured pace.
3. Smaller portions, smaller bites, chew slower, chew more.
4. Leave the table hungry, no after meal eating parties.
5. Go to bed empty.
6. Try to fast once a week at least twenty four hours (to get better at rule one).
7. Vegetables as bulk fruits, lean proteins and complex carbohydrates in moderation, fats as condiments.
8. Resist the sirens' song of sugar and refined carbo hydrate pastes, including yeast infected refined carbohydrate pastes.
9. Attract a positive self-image, make my bed.
10. Attract wellness, take my probiotics and vitamins, Tai Chi frequently.
11. Forgive imperfection in myself, those around me and life in general, admire persistence.
12. Attract and accentuate positive things to my life
13. Repeat the rules getting up and going to bed until they are part of my inner me.
14. Weigh in, successful diets need feedback (neutral attitude please)!

GET, STAY, LIKE AND DO THINGS HUNGRY AS LONG AND OFTEN AS POSSIBLE.

My rule of rules, the heart of the regime. I want to do "stuff" hungry and try to like it. What do I mean but stuff? Virtually everything! I have gotten into such a habit over the years of eating before, during and after just about everything and anything I do. I eat before exercise (a terrible idea). I snack before the dog walk and eat at work before I begin to work. I love to eat at night watching the tube. I like a bedtime snack and a three in the morning munchies run. My eating behavior has generalized to the point that hunger doesn't trigger my eating everything around me does.

Time to imitate the hunter-gatherer days of old back when hunger had to wait impatiently while the meal was caught, cleaned and cooked. Hunger is no joke, hunger is powerful. My inner animal sees, rationalizes and pounces in an instant. I need to ignore the triggers, and not let my hand to mouth compulsion betray me. I swear sometimes food is in my mouth and on its way to my stomach before I am consciously aware that I ate it! I am seriously that good (and that compulsive) at eating.

I want to be seriously good at hunger. Am I strong enough to smell freshly baked bread without eating some? I will be salivating for it, I will be rationalizing, convincing myself one slice won't hurt, knowing deep down inside the "slice" will be half the loaf before I'm through. The beast will be pacing, he will be wanting, he will most definitely be craving and gnawing in anticipation. Patience has never been his virtue, persistence is! I have to be stronger than he, I must tame him so that he turns from adversary to companion. I have to kind of, sort of, like him. It isn't easy, hunger, the oldest god is nobody's bitch.

PREP, PLATE, SIT AND EAT MY MEALS AT A SLOW AND MEASURED PACE.

My culinary career has turned me into a grazer. Chefs work when normal people eat and we constantly taste in between as we prepare for the next meal service. This has turned the three meals a day of my youth into one. The trouble is, it lasts all day. A constant stream of calories that ebbs and flows but never stops. I've gotten to a point, especially in the busy season where I just see food and eat it hungry or not. The infamous "Seefood" diet. My connection between hunger and food gets totally lost for months at a time and that is a recipe for dieting disaster. I need to get back to eating meals that have a beginning and end. I need to *prep* (prepared the meal) while hungry without picking, *plate* (my meal) like a civilized person, not eat it out of the cooking pot over a garbage can like a chef, *sit* (somewhere else then the kitchen), pause for a moment and tell the beast to calm the f**k down, and *eat at a measured pace*, despite my omnipresent desire to wolf it all down.

SMALLER PORTIONS, SMALLER BITES, CHEW SLOWER, CHEW MORE.

I have an undergraduate degree in Psychology which I am going too inflicted upon you at this time. My college specialized in the study of Behavioral Psychology (not

Freudian or Jungian and the like). Behavioral Psychology differs by only studying what can be physically measured and not delving into the mysteries of the mind and feelings. It studies behavior and how external (meaning something in the environment) "reinforcing stimuli" effect that behavior. The basic premise is: A behavior followed by a reinforcing stimulus increases in frequency. Gambling is a good example. I bet, I win (sometimes) and each time I win the desire to gamble increases so I gamble more, but a good behavioral scientist would never use the term "desire" in his description.

There are five types of reinforcing stimuli if I remember correctly. I can't name them all at the moment college was forty years ago but the one I want to talk about, the one all we fatties love, is food! So to rephrase: Any act, followed by food increases in frequency. My epiphany was, since eating is a behavior that is always followed by food the act of eating is self-reinforcing! My eating always speeds up during the meal and I always want to keep eating after the meal is finished. My behavior, eating, was rewarded by food and my inner me is chomping at the bit to keep that going. I just love after meal eating parties!

But it even gets worse. Another type of reinforcing stimulus is a "Negatively Reinforcing Stimulus". This external stimulus compels behavior by its removal. An example is moving out of the sun into the shade. The sun is the "negatively reinforcing stimulus" that compels the behavior of moving to the shade. Hunger compels in the same way. In response to hunger I eat, hunger is the negatively reinforcing stimulus that compels me to eat and as I do, I positively reinforce that behavior to keep eating. It is a wonder that everyone isn't fat. We the fat challenged, the big boned, the tribe of the triple-xers are getting a behavioral one two punch that keeps our beloved fork to mouth relationship thriving!

Generalization, another behavioral psych concept, is germane as well. Generalization of behavior happens when a stimulus, sort of migrates, effecting behaviors at a time other than it originally did. Or it could expand by pairing with other behaviors it was not originally connected to. I suffer generalization, for example, by eating in anticipation of hunger when I used to eat because of hunger. So what does all this have to do with smaller bites, chewing slower and chewing more?

I once wrote a paper for a Social Psychology Class, called the Tran-situational Man vs. the Social Animal. The Social Animal was the title the textbook we used so I thought it was a good suck up to the professor. I postulated that the only time we are "really" human is when we do not take the path of least resistance when we get out of ourselves and do what DOES'NT come natural. Living and reacting to reinforcing stimuli is natural, we are primates doing what primates do. We eat, have sex, hunt and fight so we can have even more sex and food.

I am at my best version of human when I apply my intellect to my eating. When I eat "mindfully" I am on the human side of the reinforcing curve. I rule eating it doesn't rule me. I am at my most human, when I take the road "less traveled by" as the poet Robert Frost once wrote. No more "wolfing down" food (notice the term itself is a comparison to an animals). I want to slow down, chew more, and chew slower ignoring my inner beast who is down there impatiently pouting!

I have an idea for an invention, (I don't know how to invent, I am a chef darn it) that I call the eating metronome. I want a cell phone app or a pen-like object with two small lights. One beats at a time interval that can be varied, a bite every ten, fifteen or thirty seconds for example and another that divides the first time period into twenty smaller periods.

The first tells me when to take a bite of food, the latter regulates how fast I chew. The lights should be discrete so I can place the device on the table in front of me without raising the curiosity of my fellow diners. I set the time and eat accordingly. If I talk or miss a pulse I just wait for the next. As I get comfortable with the chosen speed (some say a habit takes thirty days to learn) I then I increase the time period from let's say ten seconds to twelve and gradually slow down my eating using the feedback. This by the way, is another behavioral psych concept called "Prompt and Fade".

A shout out to my professors at Florida Southern College, thanks! See I was listening some of the time. A note to mom and dad. All that money you spent on my college education didn't entirely go to "pot" (but most of my weekly allowance did). Note to readers: If I got anything wrong from a scientific perspective please ask my Profs at F.S.C. heck I was stoned half the time and it was forty years ago college was great!

LEAVE THE TABLE HUNGRY, RESIST AFTER MEAL EATING PARTIES.

I am getting better at arriving to the table hungry but my beast takes hold about halfway through so I still need to work on leaving it that way. This behavioral "path of least resistance" is hard to break, generalization rearing its ugly head one more time. I want to live on the hungry side of life! If I keep going back for more I am giving in to my inner me and the pleasure of food. I must change who I am to change what I am.

So many habits so little time. I want to eat at a slow, measured, civilized pace and when the food on my plate is gone the meal is done. No second helpings and no trips to the fridge for "après" meal treats. I have gained a lot of respect for those civilized and structured dinners of old depicted in movies and books. Back then etiquette and civility were prized by society. I laughed at the ceremony and discipline of those affairs in my youth but I appreciate now how disciplined the first civilized people were as they tried to differentiate themselves from the primitive world from which they had most recently evolved.

Table manners are a human quality, let us all get back to using them. Dining in the twenty first century has devolved into a mindless grazing affair that has to compete with television and cell phone. We need to put the phone down and turn the television off. We should sit down at a properly set table and eat in a slow and civilized manner. It is hard to do in these busy times and hard to do when we are eating alone but it would be nice if well-defined meals became part of our daily routine once again. Heck we could even start having conversations another endangered social art. There is conversation after texting.

GO TO BED EMPTY

I am a late night food junkie. I used blame marijuana, but I ate just as much after I stopped (ok severely reduced) smoking. Late night food is comfort food, late night food is company, food me and the T.V. a ménage aux trois of hedonistic delight. We were made for each other. The theory that late night calories are worse than daytime calories has been discredited but going to bed too full has drawbacks.

As I have aged, certain body parts do not function as well as they did when I was young (That reminds me, refill the Viagra) oh I am just teasing! Viagra is fun though, read my *Thankyou Big Pharma* poem to see what I mean. The part of my anatomy germane to our conversation is the lower esophageal sphincter, gateway to the stomach. It is not as sexy as my sexy but is sure is important to my happy.

As I have fattened, my years of joyful gluttony have weakened it and now after an eating orgy, food leaks back out into my esophagus from my overfull stomach when I lie down. This unfortunate "reversal of fortunes" (a term made famous in the annual Nathan's hot dog eating contest) results in some rather uncomfortable coughing seizures when I go to bed. Not a good way to wake up. The stomach acid esophageal burn is a gluttonous perk I seek to avoid as well. Now I go to bed empty, not necessarily ravenously hungry but empty.

TRY TO FAST ONCE A WEEK AT LEAST 24 HOURS (TO GET BETTER AT RULE ONE)

Fasting is hard, fasting is controversial (**check with your doctor before trying please**). Some experts say not to, it slows down metabolism others say do it, it strengthens the immune system. Both may be true but both are irrelevant as to why I want to fast. I want to increase my ability to co-exist with the discomfort of hunger and there is no better way to do it than fasting.

Fasting "mindfully" is important as well. The time periods immediately before and after the fast are dangerous. Before I begin, my demon called rationalization takes hold as I convince myself to have a little "pre-fast" culinary fun. What harm could it be after all, I will make up for my excessive caloric intake during my period of depravation. Of course one bite leads to another and I end up waddling into my fast full to the gills and not feel hungry until I am well into it, which defeats the purpose.

Afterwards hunger, my frenemy, will be especially grumpy about its treatment. My gluttonous compulsion will strike in an instant after the mental "aw it is ok just a little won't hurt" rationalization pops into consciousness. One "taste" turns into a hand to mouth blur if I am not mindful. I can eat a days' worth of calories in about five minutes or less without coming up for air. I am good at gluttony, I have been doing it for years.

I am fasting to increase my ability to tolerate and live with hunger. I am saying "no" to the mindset that wants me to ravenously consume. I look at how my dog inhales his dinner. That is natural, all dogs "wolf" down their food. I want the opposite of that, I want human, I want my intellect to triumph over my animal. I want to own my hunger for a period of time. I want to begin and end my fast mindfully to increase my tolerance of and control over my primitive. This is a terribly hard rule to follow. I would say to date I am successful maybe twenty percent of the time. I get to around twenty hours pretty consistently but those last four are elusive.

VEGATABLES AS BULK, FRUITS, LEAN PROTEINS AND COMPLEX CARBOHYDRATES IN MODERATION, FAT AS A CONDIMENT.

I once asked a friend after he lost a good bit of weight how did he do it?

"Lots of Salads." Came the reply.

Talk about a softball question. I KNOW how to diet. All diets except for Atkins and protein sparing fasts are basically the same, lots a veggies, moderate fruits and lean proteins with carbs and fat scarce or not at all. That is how I get to the diet "Zone" that is how I "Weight Watch". That is what I got five hundred calories of on that draconian HCG diet.

Dieting is a drab world, it is how we ate back during the "hunting and gathering" period of humanity. We are still hunter/gatherers in the modern era, we "hunt" for doughnuts at Dunkin and "gather" breakfast at Mickie D's. Same behavior, disastrously fatty results, we need to pair the behavior from then with the food that was available back in that day as well, which of course is vegetables, lean proteins, fruits and some fat.

Back in the hunter/gatherer period of our human existence, there was no candy (except honeycomb), no pastries and no fun calorically dense but nutritionally challenged bar food. Food wasn't "stepped on" by our massive food industrial complex. There was no par-boiled, re-dried, vitamins re-added (because we boiled them all out) converted rice. The flour wasn't refined, bleached and bromated. Sugar wasn't ubiquitous. I can remember in my lifetime when Coca Cola came in a pre-supersized era eight ounce bottle. Bagels weighed two ounces when I was a child, now they weigh five. Why am I fat? I know why I'm fat! How do I get thin? By eating like we used to, it might be boring but it is what the human body was designed to do. I got to get me some of those roots and berries that Yogi the Bear didn't seem to enjoy either. Yogi liked pic-a-nic baskets he was a very human bear.

Dieting isn't rocket science it's just boring, I feel better when I eat "clean" a term a friend of mine likes to use. Funny how eating like our ancestors ate is now call eating "clean". My digestive system is designed to break down and derive nutrition from plants and animals, not the yeast infected refined carbohydrate pastes we all love. My next rule is all about those wonderfully dangerous things.

RESIST THE SIRENS' SONG OF SUGAR & REFINED CARBOHYDRATE PASTES INCLUDING YEAST INFECTED REFIND CARBOHYDRATE PASTES.

The Sirens, creatures in ancient Greek mythology, were both beautiful and dangerous. They lived on an island in the Mediterranean Sea luring sailors to shipwreck by singing an irresistibly enchanting song. According to Wikipedia:

"Their (the Sirens) song, though irresistibly sweet, was no less sad than sweet, and lapped both body and soul in a fatal lethargy, the forerunner of death and corruption. The term "siren song" refers to an appeal that is hard to resist but that, if heeded, will lead to a bad conclusion."

Now what dietetically, does that sound like? Can we all say sugar? I know we can! I know sugar up close and personal one of my pastry displays will shipwreck my diet every time, eclairs, napoleons and tarts oh my! Sugar in my opinion is as much drug as food. It is sugar cane juice reduce to a syrup and refined to a powder. Maybe that doctor I spoke about earlier was right, sugar is like cocaine similar process different plant! It taste's a lot better, rats given a choice of sugar or cocaine choose sugar every time.

Some studies suggest an over consumption of sugar causes a candida overgrowth in our intestinal tracts. Candida is a yeast that is part our guts natural bacterial flora but studies suggest excessive sugar consumption causes its overgrowth and that has health implications. Google it and judge for yourself. The overgrowth is self-perpetuating as well, increasing sugar cravings in the person that has it, it sure does that to me.

I do love my sugar but sadly it is time to steer away from the dietetic shipwreck that the siren song of sugar will surely cause. I want to set course for the fresh, calm, "clean" sea of vegetables, lean proteins and fruit! Hmmm…let me try that again, set a course for the fresh calm, "clean" sea of vegetables, lean proteins and fruit! Nope it didn't do it for me that time either, it just doesn't get me going. It has about as much appeal as kissing my sister.

The thought of a crème caramel makes my heart sing, the thought of broccoli makes both my esophageal and anal sphincters twitch. I have always maintained that before God kills you he takes away your vices one by one. He is most certainly doing that to me and my love of food. I find it unfair and I am going to write a strongly worded letter to him regarding the matter.

I had an epiphany recently. As a child we made paste from flour and water. Yes we made it, gorilla glue had yet to be invented. Recently, it came to me that if I added some yeast and salt to that old fashioned paste I'd have bread! White bread is nothing more than a yeast infected flour paste, an unappetizing description for such a ubiquitous food, everyone loves bread it is an enticing Siren.

I LOVE white bread, especially crusty French baguettes. My first job in the workday during my culinary apprenticeship was to unwrap and melt two big cases of butter in an even bigger tall pot, in an absolutely huge steam table that resided in the hotels main kitchen. Serendipitously the daily French bread delivery would arrive from the boulangerie (French Bakery) still warm from the ovens. Talk about a "Sirens song" the aroma of fresh baked bread is so compelling.

A few of us got into the habit of taking a loaf (they were about two feet long and two inches in diameter) and plunging it into the huge pot of melted butter and then eating them like a popsicle. Oh my god it was SO good! The gluttony of my youth, I miss it so. To make a long story short, one loaf became two and the fat started to bloom. We all had to stop but O.M.G. they were so good! Culinary fun seems to have a relationship that is inversely proportional to health. The carefree days of my youth are gone and it is time to emphasize healthy eating over the pleasure of a butter drenched Baguette.

ATTRACT A POSITIVE SELF IMAGE, MAKE THE BED!

My many pejorative self-chat "why can't I lose weight" beat downs have taken a toll on my self-image over the years and thought precedes result. A video named *The Secret* impressed this on me, I recommend viewing it. The video is about "The law of Attraction" and how the way I think precedes and attracts physical world results. Negative "I don't want" thinking produces negative results and I was guilty of that in spades. For example thinking,

"I don't want bills in the mail" or getting mad when seeing bills in the mail and thinking "damn it more bills" gets more bills in the mail!

Changing the internal/mental/emotional conversation to

"I will to get checks in the mail" (Even if there were bills in the mailbox) would attract checks. It isn't a perfect example but that is the general idea.

So relative to weight loss, does thinking "I need to lose weight" attract more weight to lose? Am I attracting fat? I am now trying to change my inner conversation to attract thinness. I want to think, I like empty, I like hungry and hungry is healthy. I want to get on the scale thinking thin thoughts and not I hope I lost some weight thoughts. I don't want the weight I "lost" to find its way back home again! I want to attract what I desire not what I don't!

All well and good you say, but what does this have to do with making the bed? Recently I read an article about a Navy Seal Commander giving a college commencement speech. He spoke to the graduates of his seal training and how the first thing they did each day was to make their "rack" which is what navy guys call a bed. He said making the bed started his day with a successful task and whether the day went well or badly, he came back to nicely made bed. That act and the attitude towards it, produced positive results and a positive self-image.

I decided to act on the commander's advice as I am not a great bed maker. I found it does make me feel better. It starts my day with a nice feeling (that goes out to infinity attracting good things) and after my day is done good or bad, there it is well made and looking good! Investing in my self-image, taking care of myself, being an advocate for myself, looking in the mirror and liking what looks back is important. I have a kind heart, I am a good person and it is time to emphasize that. When I dwell on the misery of obesity I do nothing but attract it. I need to get off this roller coaster of negativity and like what I see. Self-affirmation will attract good things.

ATTRACT WELLNESS TAKE MY PROBIOTICS AND VITAMINS, TAI CHI FREQUENTLY.

I miss the good old days when I could eat butter without fear of imminent death. Now we suffer the constant drone of modern science regarding its evils. If I butter my toast, I am so going to die! Heck just being fat puts me at risk of imminent death. My achy back? I'm too fat! My feet ache? Too much weight over those poor things. Blood pressure too high? Too damn fat! Fat shaming is in and it is so unfair. I am surrounded by thin people constantly complaining about their backs, feet and blood pressure and have yet to hear anyone say it from them being too skinny.

All this "fat as a death sentence" conversation messes with my head so I better change something! Starting my day with vitamins and probiotics is a positive affirmation that my body is a temple! A big sumptuous, fluffy temple yes, but a temple none the less. My morning vitamins are an internal version of "making my bed" as discussed above. No matter how my day goes, taking my vitamins, minerals and probiotics each morning gives me a positive psychological and physiological start to my day.

Back in the long gone days of my youth we were closer to the land and farms that grew our food. As the years passed and demand grew, our now giant food-industrial complex replaced the family farms. Food quantity has gone up, but its quality down in my opinion.

As I a Chef I do know this subject quite well. Modern tomatoes look great but lack taste and aroma, egg shells once thick are now paper thin, red delicious apples once crisp and sweet, are now mealy and tasteless. Animal husbandry has become so bad I pay more for chickens raised in a good environment and am more careful about buying packaged steaks and ground beef since most now are gassed with carbon monoxide to preserve their appetizing appearance well after their freshness date has expired.

No wonder we slather our vegetables with fatty dressings, add sugar to our green picked and shipped from afar fruit and eat chemically enhanced snacks in our modern calorically abundant but nutritionally challenged world. Now I take vitamins and spend more for quality food, I want to attract wellness and what we put in our bodies has a lot to do with that very thing.

Exercise has and always will be an important part of wellness. It used to be ingrained in our existence but the modern world has replaced the peripatetic journey of our hunter/gather past with a sedentary modern version of life that takes place in front of our computer and television screens. An old guy once told me,

"If you keep moving it is harder for them to get the last nail in the coffin."

We fatties aren't the only ones with gallows humor old people have it as well. Fat and old a double scoop of blessings from the infinite to me. Now that I am both expect my next book to be extremely sarcastic! My body is beginning to fall apart faster than I can repair it but the one thing I do know, I need to keep moving. Use it or lose it is the reality of senior living.

I've tried different forms of exercise, I found weight lifting boring and aerobics undignified so I settled on Tai Chi which is the most popular exercise in the world. It seems that anything a gazillion Chinese people do ends up the most popular thing in the world (at least that is what my instructor told me). Tai Chi has the caloric burn of walking and is great for balance and flexibility. Its complexity is interesting and it can be done at home, which for me, a time challenged culinary professional is a plus, no trips to the gym needed. In aerobics class the women behind me just kept giggling I felt just like a piece of meat with those brutes. Use it or lose it and use it to lose it, exercise helps in so many ways!

FORGIVE IMPERFECTION AND ADMIRE PERSISTENCE IN MYSELF THE PEOPLE AROUND ME AND LIFE IN GENERAL.

It took me forty years to reach my fatty peak, hopefully it won't take that long to get back to a thinner me, but forty years of bad habits aren't changed overnight. There will be failures, I will fall off plan, that is the reality. There will be imperfections in the people around me and life in general as well. It could be a holiday, a new girlfriend or work stress. It might be a celebration like a wedding or something sad like the death of a loved one. All these events trigger the urge to fall back to old habits that comfort and console and my best of friend food is always close by. Dietetic procrastination and rationalization are big with me as well. The oldest excuse in my diet avoidance manual is,

"One last meal before I get back on plan!"

Those last meals add up! I had a running joke with my colleagues.

"What is the best day to go on a diet?" I would ask rhetorically.

"Tomorrow!" I would answer.

My buddy the beast is always with me waiting for a chance to roam the Elysium fields of caloric pleasure. Before the rules, I would give myself a mental flogging that was invariably followed by total dietetic capitulation after a binge. A self-defeating cycle of attracting the negative! All fat shamers out there take heart, we fatties are our own worst critics. It is time this fat challenged human gets off my psychological roller coaster of shame. If I blow the rules, no dwelling, no pouting, no bouts of recrimination, I now forgive myself and get back to following the rules as quickly as I can.

Forgiveness applies the people around me as well. Staying angry at someone, leads to "hangry" a rationalization for a nice little pity party of caloric consumption that always ends in self-recrimination and a pejorative mental rant. You know the drill by now, just avoid it, forgive that person. If I get mad at my girlfriend and eat blaming her (I am so good at that) the responsibility for my fork to mouth compulsion is mine not hers.

I am human and imperfect, as are we all. Negative thought produces negative attraction, forgive. Fate will throw tough times my way I need to soldier through them. A partial following of the rules helped maintain my weight during some hard times I recently experienced and that in itself is a great success! Accentuate the positive and admire persistence. Those are the qualities that will help me succeed at changing who I am and that will change what I am!

ATTRACT AND ACCENTUATE POSITIVE THINGS TO MY LIFE

I added this rule because I didn't want to have thirteen rules. I remember making fun of my Mom as a child when she said they shouldn't have named the thirteenth Apollo mission to the moon "Apollo 13" before its launch. Then it blew up in outer space and we almost lost the Astronauts. That gave me pause. As they said in *"The Secret"* video (I recommend it) there is more to life than we can see, we are not just a bunch of meat suits walking around.

When I think of this rule, something inside of me brightens, I can't explain it but I do like to attract it. Good things are going to happen dear reader, this book I am writing is going to be a great success! A great day at work will be had by all! Good things are coming! Reading that makes you feel better right? Well not about my book but the rest.

Positive thought, produces positive feelings which in turn attracts positive things. When you repeat this rule try to get that feeling, it is always a good moment in my day, I hope it will be in yours as well!

REPEAT THE RULES GETTING UP AND GOING TO BED

I repeat the rules at the beginning and end each day. I want to integrate them into my psychology so they pop up at critical points during my dieting day when a choice is to be made. They are the intellectual life preserver in my caloric ocean. They are my chance to take the right path. When my hand reaches for that cookie, I want to hear in my mind,

"Resist the siren song of sugar."

Giving myself a chance to make the right call, put the cookie back and eat something more healthful or better yet, not eat at all. When I feel the urge to pick at food while cooking I want to hear,

"Prep, plate, sit and eat."

I want to keep my inner beast at bay through the good

offices of my human will. The rules are my framework for a thinner, happier, healthier life. The rules are my "boy on the elephant" riding herd on my primitive. All I have to do is follow them. They're not magic and hunger will ALWAYS try and get its way. The only diet that works hundred percent of the time is the grave. That reminds me I want, "Finally a diet that works!" written on my gravestone.

WEIGH IN, SUCCESSFUL DIETS NEED FEEDBACK (NEUTRAL ATTITUDE PLEASE!)

To say I dislike the scale, that merciless arbiter of my self-worth, is an understatement. A cook I once terminated and saw again long after summed up my attitude toward the scale in one sentence.

"I've been thinking a lot about you Chef and none of it's been good."

That is exactly how I feel about the scale! But (Insert a really petulant sigh.) it ain't a diet if I don't weigh in! I have read more than once, the one dieting behavior that helps with weight loss most consistently is weighing in. No wonder my inner child wants to avoid it so desperately. But feedback is necessary or a cycle of eating and scale avoidance takes over.

I have compromised with the judge in the bathroom; I weigh in once a week, a daily weigh in make me crazy, a pound up a pound down, I did well today, oops no I didn't what the "F***!? Once a week, on Mondays, that works for me. Before I step onto the loathsome thing I repeat, neutral attitude, neutral attitude in my head and hopefully I will have one, no guarantees. Talk about attracting the negative my attitude is atrocious!

Along with my good buddy the scale (sounds better but I am still not feeling it) I like try on a shirt that is a little too small as well. If scale doesn't move but I feel thinner the shirt will show it. Sometimes muscle replaces fat. Some use a tape measure to track and I am all for it if it comes with a cute little female diet technician to help me do it. The bottom line is feedback is necessary and the cute diet tech is a luxury.

On a side note I have changed my mind about weight loss itself. I am in favor of slow thinning instead of quick. A harder path to be sure, my fantasy has always been, movie star thin in less than three months. But I have become suspicious that a correlation between losing weight fast and gaining it back quicker exists. I lost ninety five pounds on a protein sparing fast in three months. Three months of protein drinks and nothing else, it wasn't pretty. At the end I looked down at a thigh that just wasn't mine, it looked anorexic, it was someone else's. The quick weight loss resulted in a sort of body dysmorphia, my inner me, did not like me at all. I gained it all back plus some, in less than 5 months.

My change of mind has been vindicated just recently. There was a study on the alumni of "The Biggest Loser" television show. I never liked the show and did not watch it after seeing one personal trainer actually place his foot onto the stomach of a very obese and exhausted guy prostrate on the floor telling him to suck it up and get back to exercising. Torturing fatties while the world watched was how I saw the series. Jillian Michaels should have dressed up in leather, I would have probably watched it then she was so attractive to me in both physique and attitude! You know that old chefly saying,

"Chefs do it with whips!" I know, I know my male mind is in the gutter yet again but THAT is what male minds do.

Heck, I thought Sofia Vergara's name was Sofia Viagra for about six months before one of my colleagues corrected me. I saw the beauty that is her, got to the "V" in her last name and my libido took over!

The results of the study after tracking the contestants for six years after appearing on the show were dismal. Scientists found that after such an intensive period of weight loss the dieter's body tries to actively gain the weight back for up to SIX YEARS. Six frigging (I am thinking f**king rest assured) years! They found that the body actually lowered its metabolic rate to facilitate weight gain. For one man they tracked, the amount of calories that he ate at the beginning of the show to lose weight was now the amount he needed to maintain after he had gained one hundred pounds of what he had lost back. HUNGER IS NOBODYS BITCH!

It took me fifty years to accumulate my fluffy folds. The idea that I can lose them in a year or less is ridiculous fantasy. Changing who and what I am in context of the ebb and flow of my life is what is needed. I have to acquire new habits during the fun of vacations, the stressful times at work and even during visits by the "in-laws" (forget it eat, it's the in-laws). If I change enough I hope to reach a tipping point where I lose more than I gain during my year, ending it thinner instead of fatter. This is the dietetic sweet spot I am struggling towards. This is what I am trying to attract.

CONCLUSION

A lifestyle that tilts the scale from gaining more than I lose to losing more than I gain. The choice always there and will always be mine. Hunger has become the precious commodity in the modern times that we live. It is hunger I must cultivate and a stubborn primal mind that I must tame. I need to replace negative with positive, attracting what I want. I want hungry. I want thinner. I want emptiness. The feeling of hunger is the feeling of health. The feeling of hunger is the path to a healthier, thinner me.

One thing is for certain. This approach has me feeling, lighter (scale or not) more energetic and more optimistic. I am presently down around fifty pounds from my lifetime peak. The yoyo gain/loss cycle has ameliorated from a seventy pound annual spread, to twenty. Next year I hope to get it to zero, no net gain at all during the year what a blessing that would be. Starting my summer diet from zero gained rather than a deficit, would be SO great! If I change my habits, I change my life.

I titled the book "The Dieters Companion" because that is what it is, a companion, to amuse while you lose, entertain if you gain and hopefully enlighten so you'll lighten! I am a chef and not a scientist but come on, life experience has to count for something and the boffin's track record on obesity cures is not exactly stellar.

No matter what weight loss program or diet you choose, I hope it helps with a "been there done that" empathy to brighten that long and sometimes bumpy road to thinness. I feel for you my lap band of brothers (and of course dear sisters of the traveling plus size pant suit) and wish you success, in life, love and loss! Weight loss that is! Best of wishes and best of luck!.

...and Remember!

A DIET IS MERELY AN INTELLECTUAL REGIME GOVERNING THE PRIMAL IMPERATIVE OF HUNGER AND APPETITE THAT WILL ALWAYS WANTS TO TOPPLE IT.

I will never ever "want" to diet. I will always "want" to eat. Dieting is an intellectual decision. Dieting is mind over fatter. By the way did you catch the "merely" up there? It means we dieters are out gunned, we have to be on guard twenty four seven, three sixty five. Hunger is at best a grumpy roommate.

THE CHOICE IS ALWAYS HUNGRY OR DEPRESSED AND I'D RATHER BE HUNGRY!

When I overeat or binge I feel guilty. That leads to a pejorative self-rant that ends in depression, which I ameliorate by eating, leading to more guilt, another mental beat ending in more depression which of course I alleviate with more food! Stop the merry go round I want to get off! I would rather be hungry!

I MUST CHANGE WHO I AM TO CHANGE WHAT I AM

The rules aren't a diet, they are a change in focus. Being what I was, a fun food free grazing couch potato who occasionally went on draconian diets got me what I am, fatter! The diet must become part of the ebb and flow and fabric of my life. During the good times and bad, for better or worse, in sickness and in health, till death do we part! I am married to it! Jeeez that's depressing I'm cruising to fridge I'll be right back.

I WANT MY BELLY TO BE PART OF ME NOT ALL OF ME

This bad boy will take over if I let it and what makes him happy in his world makes me miserable in mine. Exercise my core more! When this rule pops into my head, I start tensing and relaxing my stomach until I feel it while walking the dog or driving the car. I don't need to be one hundred sit ups crazy (though all power to you if you can). I just need to be persistent in the struggle with my fluffy foe.

NOTHING TASTES AS GOOD AS THIN FEELS

I want to accentuate my human by choosing the deferred reward of health and thinness over the immediate gratification and pleasure of food. I want to choose "The road less traveled by" over "the path of least resistance". The hard way is the human way. The hard road leads to where I want to go.

We accentuate our "human" when we override our primal instincts with the power of intellect. Feeling thin is feeling energetic. Feeling thin is tying my shoes without busting a capillary in my forehead. Feeling thin is lightening the load over my suffering knees. Feeling thin, feels pretty darn good.

CHOOSE AND EAT MINDFULLY

I excel at eating mindlessly, no thought, just a contented staccato fork to mouth rhythm. When I get outside of myself and observe I can't help but be impressed. I am so good at consuming mega calories in a very short period of time. But to get and stay thinner, I need to eat "mindfully" for dieting is a behavioral aberration that requires constant mental engagement.

I want to buy healthy at the store and resist impulse buys (that "last chance to be bad" array of treats at the cash register? Sorry pal verboten!). I want to prepare a slow cooked, healthy meal in the presence of hunger without picking. I want to plate, sit and eat that meal at a slow and measured pace despite hunger urging me faster. I want to finish the meal without engaging in an "after meal" eating party. Mindless eating got me here, mindful eating gets me back.

REMEMBER, I AM DETERMINED TO...

I like to give myself projects each day to help me improve a weaknesses in my life. I am a scatter brained air head and the repetition helps me focus. The thoughts may be related to my hunger rules or could be in another area of my life like writing a section of this book. I pick a weak point and work on it.

I am determined to, finish a section of my book. I am determined to, stay hungry for an hour before I eat at work. A Chef once told me that unless I was constantly trying to get better, I would just become worse nothing ever stays the same. He was so right, but then again, The Chef is ALWAYS right!

Ponderously Pondering Silly Fats
...I mean Facts!
(All I know is what I read on the net)

If Einstein thought about it...

Einstein the famed physicist said energy can neither be created nor destroyed. Well fat is stored energy is it not? Therefore it can't be either! Which means it is a constant that is just moved around.

So be happy! If you gain weight, you have saved a fellow human from that fate and if you want to lose you can try to fatten all your friends and increase your chances of success!

If Darwin thought about it...

Dieting is intellectual governance over antediluvian impulses and instincts so compelling and evolutionarily successful that they are the reason we are in the here and now bitching about how hard it is to lose weight.

When God thinks about it (Judeo-Christian)

"He that is of a proud heart stirreth up strife: but he that putteth his trust in the LORD shall be made fat. " Proverbs 28:25

Sounds pretty good but then again

"I will seek that which is lost, and bring again that which was driven away, and will bind up that which was broken, and will strengthen that which was sick: but I will destroy the fat and the strong; I will feed them judgment." Ezekiel 34:16

God sounds undecided but anyone who got fat at the church social is probably safe.

The Etymology of "Diet"

Well let's see….there's *Die* and *it*! Am I dying to eat it? Am I going to die because of it? Will I die if I don't follow it? So not good! Diet is from the Greek word "diatia" which means "way of life". Personally I like my thoughts on the subject better, at least I don't give you a life sentence (just the possibility of premature death).

Silly Fats...

A report on Public Broadcast Radio said people who drank tea, specifically Oolong or green were less fat than those that didn't. I am a coffee guy I would rather die young than drink green tea!

I read not getting enough sleep causes the hormones that trigger hunger to elevate. In my opinion, it is the three in the morning munchies run that have trained my hunger hormones to elevate.

If eating green foods help with my diet does pistachio ice cream count?

A recent scientific study showed that obesity is socially contagious like a virus. Just knowing a fat person or being a friend of a friend of a fat person increases the chances that you will become fat! I am the Typhoid Mary of obesity.

A study on rats (the animal, not a person of low character or a lawyer) in England showed that a high fat "American Style" diet coupled with stress (which for the poor rats meant an electric shock every minute) produced extremely obese rats. Finally productive diet science. This knowledge would be so good for breeding, after all rats are eaten in China and were for a period of time, a delicacy in France called "Coopers Balontine."*

*To be fair it was a delicacy during the siege of Paris in 1870.

Those busy boffins found that the percentage of risk factors for disease and death were basically the same for thin people and us fatties. The insurance premiums weren't! (The scientists didn't observe the last part that was me.)

A most recent scientific study in rats (those poor rats) found that a combinations of two hormones with names way too hard for me to remember caused significant weight loss. In my opinion, they should give those drugs to the poor rat bastards they shocked the hell out of in that first study.

Did you ever read about the side effects of the ALLI* diet pill? Written on the side of the box is a warning about potential side effects and I quote:

"...These include loose or more frequent stools that may be hard to control, or gas with an oily discharge. The excess fat that passes out of your body is not harmful. In fact you may recognize it as

something that looks like the oil on top of a pizza."

That's right off the box real nice! They had to mention pizza where's the phone.

*ALLI is a diet pill that prevents fat from being absorbed in your intestine

During the initial outbreak of Swine Flu, the Jews and Muslims and pig farmers came together demanding that the swine flu virus's name be changed to H1N1. The Jews, Muslims and pig farmers came together in agreement on an issue. If someone told me that I would reply.

"Sure when pigs fly!" ("Swine flu" get it? Where's that drum roll when I need it!)

A few years back Pope Benedict broke his wrist from a fall. He soldiered on performing his official duties and then underwent surgery to repair the damage to his hand. The Vatican then reported that he was convalescing at his vacation home. The pope has a vacation home? Does that mean God can't call?

Being male, I have an understandably high degree of ambivalence regarding the neutering of my male dog. Guys just don't do that to other guys, I don't care what anyone says it just aren't happening to my pal. He came in with all his parts and he is hopefully leaving the same way.

All the neutering propaganda bothers me as well. For example, neutering doesn't cause its victim to get fat, the subsequent diet does. What a total crock I am a Chef pull my other leg will you!

Bulls get their balls cut off to become steers on the way to our dinner table as that beautifully "well marbled" (marble=fat!) red meat that we all love in the U.S.A.. Cut off a roosters nuts and he becomes a fat and most probably less happy capon wandering around the barnyard looking at the hens and thinking,

"Oh well, I guess will eat something." one fatty in my family is enough, it isn't happening to my dog.

While pondering this very subject on a dog walk I ran into a woman, a fellow dog walker whom I saw off and on. When told of my ambivalence she came out empathically in favor of neutering.

"He will be so much happier." she enthused "Save him from a life of tension and frustration!"

"Like he should be different than the rest of the males on the planet?" I replied

She gave me that patented female mildly appalled look so I added,

"Besides he has a Teddy Bear at home he screws."

Her disapproval went from minor to major and she walk off, but hey a guy's got to do what a guy's got to do. He has sex with his teddy and I wash it every couple of months or so whether it needs it or not, that is what we guys do.

The majority of women with whom I've conversed all seem to be enthusiastic proponents of neutering. Women are scary, but like the doomed male black widow spider I still find them ever so attractive.

If wearing black makes me look thinner, does wearing white make me look fatter? I've bought black underwear. Does that count?

The latest study says being overweight makes the mind age eight years faster than the body and if the person is obese (and I am) it ratchets up to double! That makes my brain seventy five years old, can it collect social security? I could use the money.

Researchers in London (those Brits do a lot of fat research) found that a fat person puts a ton more carbon dioxide (global warming) into the air than a thin person. I just know that they are going to tax my fat butt now please let my brain have that social security!

As a side note regarding our neighbors across the pond. When a country has food with names like Sausage Toad in the Hole, Chip Butty and Spotted Dick on their menu, obesity research will surely follow, cheers!

I was chatting with a friend while driving on the interstate about the new construction we saw. When she pointed out the brand new truck weigh in station, I thought cool finally a place I can weigh in.

Note to self, the next time I get a dog, the tail points down, if you aren't the lead dog the view never changes.

I know I'm fat when....

1. "One Size Fits All"...doesn't.
2. My "outtie" turned into an "innie".
3. I buy shoes without laces.
5. I can balance a large popcorn AND soda on my stomach "no handed" at the movies.
6. The sounds in my stomach remind me of whale song.
7. I have to lean to one side to read the bathroom scale.
8. When I lean over to eat my sandwich, I STILL get food on my shirt.
9. People keep trying to roll me back in the water at the beach.
10. It only takes a gallon of water to fill the tub after I am in.
11. My breasts are bigger than my wife's.

Poems along
The Way

Chapter 5

Puppies, Canes
And Window Panes

New Puppy Walk

An enjoyable morning walk today
just me and puppy, my Bichon Frisé.
His fur like cotton, his eyes bright coal
and he's barely aware of my control.
Puppy scampering at first light
excited for every stick in sight!
Tugging me determinedly
do I walk him or he walk me?
A bundle of joy, my fish on the line!
The cute little furry white cuddling kind!
My morning walks with my little friend
has helped to make me young again.
A happy way to start the day.
A sunrise walk with my Bichon Frisé.

The Walking Rhyme

Princey* boy do you think it's time
to recite our walking rhyme?
Is that a bark? Are you inclined?
Is that what's on your doggy mind?
A mellow trip to that world refined
of condo dwellers at dog walk time?
Come on boy, let's get some air
I'm fat, your furry, we're quite a pair
a band of brothers debonair!
Just look at that tail wagging there
a happy puppy, I do declare!
Now off we go and cats beware!

***Replace with your dog's name,
even if it's Bartholomew!**

Three Cheers for Evolution

Most of the time I think it's grand
canine play in doggie land.
I'm just grateful that in God's plan
as we evolved to modern man
He changed the greeting of our clan
from sniffing butt to shaking hands!

Doggy Dreamland

A penny for my doggy's thoughts
as I watch him in his chair
deep in doggy dreamland
far away somewhere.
I watch him lying on his back
legs running in midair
Is he dreaming of the beach?
He always liked it there.
My little fluff ball tail wags
he's barking puppy barks
maybe he is playing
at a dreamland doggy park.
Then my sweetie, he awakes
to my adoring gaze.
He runs and jumps to my embrace
I love his doggie ways.
He wags his tail and licks my face
all canine lovingly
could it be in dreamland
my doggie dreamt of me?

Teddy Bear Love
(adultish)

I fell for a woman in the days of my youth
a beauty with pet, a doggie uncouth.
One day while we were busy in bed
she said "Isn't he cute?" and I turned my head
there he was, a frisky Bichon
on top of a teddy bear and getting it on!
Prince was his name, the dog, not the bear
a crusty old pink one with the first name of Care.

He was grunting and snorting and having his way
if Princey could talk, I bet he would say...
"I'm getting some good old teddy bear love!
This pink teddy bear, she's a gift from above!
She pushes my buttons; she has the right stuff
she makes my little Princey go ruff, ruff, ruff!"

Well I fell for the girl and it didn't take long
for her to move in bringing doggie along.
While loading the car to move us down south
Prince came a running with that bear in his mouth.
He had a "Don't forget this!" look in his eye
and I busted out laughing at the smart little guy.
So I loaded it up with his balls and his bones
for canine amusement when he was alone.

Yes, Princey and I, two boys on the brink
me thinking honey and him thinking pink.
Both ruled by forces we couldn't explain
male misdirection between groin and the brain.
Deep down I think we knew it was wrong
but our heads were not listening, talk to our schlongs!

My rut finally lifted and reality set in
she wasn't my yang and I wasn't her yin.
If I said a word, she would bite off my head
sex play was out, we bought separate beds.
Hers was all girly, which was good in the end
when her shiny pink pillow became Prince's new friend.
I saw him humping it during one of our fights
and went to sleep grinning
when she turned out the light.

Epilog
"RUFFFFF you up baby? You like that?
Who's your doggy!!
WHOOO'S YOURRRR DOGEEEEE!!
Wow...that was good...what's the wets stuff?
Hmmm...tastes pretty good...
It's on me too...mmm....still tastes good!"

Franken-pup

Designer dog and Franken-pup
are modern ways to describe a mutt.
A giant poodle plus gold lab
creates a little "Star Wars" lad.
The progeny of that nookie
looks just like a mini Wookie!
A Cabapoo? Who named that mutt?
An Oenophile thought it up?
With all the pairings new out there
what's coming next in this affair?
Could we breed reality
with doggie stars seen on T.V.?
Scooby Doo, now he could sire
offspring we could all admire.
A Cockapoo and old Scooby
a brand new breed for you and me!
Colorful puppies and comics to
our band new Cock-a-poodle-doos!

**(I wanted to breed my Bichon
with a Scottish terrier, for a Biscotti!)**

A Dog's Tale
(A Fable my dog told me)

Once upon an ancient time
back when earth began it's rhyme
long before we dogs knew man
magic plagued a blighted land.
Humble elves lived in that place
chaffing under its embrace.
In their hearts God sang a song
that gave them magic, wise and strong.
That enchantment was the key
to tame an Earth he magically
created back when he was young
an earth that had to be redone.

It was an world of crimson light
volcanic fire and dragon fights.
Wizards ruled the barren land
where power corrupts as power can.
Back then your race were lowly slaves
living hopeless for all your days.
That earth created with shock and awe
where life and death were spell and claw
turned crueler with the passing time
and saddened the Almighty's mind.
This time he thought to use his heart
to temper his creative art.

But the balance had to be
altered somewhat subtlety.
It's realization would have to start
from kindness given to eleven hearts
and so it was the clever elves
fought the ancient magic's spell.
They turned the dragons into birds
made the wizards forget their words
and to help the children forget the past
they played with them until they laughed.
Then they turned their gentle hand
to the greening of the land.
They cooled the earth with rain and dew
and changed the crimson sky to blue.
They plucked a rainbow from the sky
to color birds and butterflies.

Alas the elves knew deep inside
old and new could not abide.
The ancient magic in their hearts
destined them to be apart
from the triumph of God's plan
free will and love in the heart of man.
The Eleven Queen knew all along
how the victory could go wrong.
She knew the freed could be oppressed
by the magic her elves possessed.
She knew that truth for elf and man.
Power corrupts, as power can.

She decreed they leave one day
and in the clouds, they sailed away
never to be seen again.
the ancient magic at an end
and so the old would fade to new
God took them from your memory to.
A pyrrhic victory, bittersweet
a victory that felt, just like defeat.
In their hearts along with pride
was a lonely hole, a mile wide.
Exile was a dreadful blow
but they left the land so you could grow.

Alas the elves they couldn't bear
leaving the ones for whom they cared.
Broken hearted they couldn't fight
a melancholy that gripped them tight.
and so the song that was their heart
began to fade and fall apart.
The brightness dulled in magic eyes
and the elves immortal began to die.
Their broken hearts sang songs of woe
that reached creators immortal soul.
So down from heaven he came to mend
that which troubled his beloved friends

But Atlantis, their enchanted isle
had lost its magic and become defiled.
While caring for his dying friends
God realized what had to mend
what his heart knew all along
exactly where it all went wrong.
The entirety of their noble past
didn't warm like a child's laugh
the cure was where they couldn't go
it was the humans they'd come to know.
It was the balance he had ordained
magic lost, for magic gained.

Near the palace on steps of jade
enrobed sky blue with gold brocade
stood the queen, ghostly pale
fainting as her spirit failed.
God ran to her and held her tight
then turned within with all his might
to the infinity that was his heart
searching to find that missing part
that tiny piece of balance he
moved to change reality.
To cure the magic he'd undone
and keep the magic he'd just begun.

Beyond the realm of all things known
inward past deaths somber throne
behind creations ticking clock
to a place his youth forgot.
There it dwelled with gentle glow.
that only a heart can see and know.
From creation to the end of time

it is beacon of all that's kind.
Barely conscious in his embrace
he took her spirit to that place
and gave her what you humans know
a tiny bit of a thing called soul.

He cured her sorrow with its might
dispelled her darkness with its light
the kind we find in children's laughs
on sunny days down garden paths.
The light we feel in moms embrace.
The glow we see on a child's face.
There, deep in his complexity
between creation and creativity
while stitching up both time and space
he felt her move in his embrace
in a place no human knows
hope kindled in his godly soul.

What had happened? Not even he
could grasp it intellectually!
Yet in his heart he felt the right
as they traveled back to the light.
The queen had changed to his surprise
Into a dog with golden eyes.
She barked out happily in dog
"I'm glad I didn't turn out frog!"
and for the first time, in quite a while
the Godly one began to smile.
With a thought he dispelled death's fog
and all the elves turned into dogs!

They chase their tails and ran about
long dogs, short dogs thin and stout
big and small, short haired and long
barking happy doggy songs.
And then as one they asked their friend.
"Can we see the kids again?"
Then God knew all was restored
and gave the elves their just reward.
He split the waters and sank the land
and off we ran to be with man.
The ancient magic's epitaph
was a big old happy Godly laugh.

So that is how we came to be
members of your family.
A happy accident of a plan awry
for even God eats humble pie.
But in the end he made us whole
with a touch of love and a thing called soul.
We play on Earth and heaven to
back and forth between God and you.
Our queen decided to stay on high
and can be seen in the evening sky.
It's not the moon we are barking too
but to a star twinkling bright and blue.

So on the day your doggy dies
don't be sad for up on high
God always comes to help him climb
to a place where all things rhyme.
Your furry pal's in heaven above
lolling in clouds and feeling the love.
Remember human, that in the end
dogs always can be pups again.
when you look in a puppies eyes
what looks back is old and wise
and maybe, just maybe when looking again
You just might see, a new, old friend.

**When I expressed my doubts about the tale,
my dog Prince took offense
"What's DOG spelled backwards?" He asked.
He hasn't spoken a word since. Afterwards I
thought darn, a talking dog? Maybe it was true.
So I've given him even more treats
and hugs ever since!**

A Tall Florida Tale

Arrr!!! Buy me a rum lads and I'll tell ye a tale
a chillin' description of a season of gales.
'Twas right where we're sitting, back in '04
when four hell spawned demons battered our shores.
Hurricanes friend, they be tricky and cruel
the meanest bastards the devil can brew.
Aye, for the price of a nice shot o' rum
I'll tell of the summer that made me a bum.

The first storm be Charley, cursed be his name
the herald 'twas he of that summer profane.
He be moving so quick and changing so fast
they miscalled his landfall, the disaster be cast.
More tornado than cane his wind field tight
Punta Gorda ambushed in the dark of the night.
He beat that town like a Bahamian beats conch
took it right down to below the sidewalks.
Old trees he pillaged and ripped out like weeds
The houses he plundered were blown out to sea.
Aye, believe it or not, but I swear it be true
that devil cane Charley cut an island in two.

Then came ol' Frances she stay out at sea
building her strength afore coming for me.
A kraken at landfall she covered the state
and becalmed in the water and sealed my fate.
She pounded away for a day and a night.
She was so massive she ate all the light!
I swear it be true, I be there, it's a fact
she gave me respect for the color PITCH BLACK!
Her winds were demonic and determined to find
a way to my fear, clawing mansion and mind.
Her winds kept increasing, in the midst of the roar
there came a knock, knocking on the front of my door.
Aye a knocking I say, not a rattle or shake
the very same sound your crewmate would make
if the poor bastard was out caught in that storm
that she-devil baited me that way until morn.

Then Ivan came callin' with a terrible force
Ropes end the West Indies with Florida on course.
A devil on Cayman he dug from the ground
the dearly departed and blew them through town.
They be hung up on fences and impaled on trees
And the wind got them dancing for loved ones to see.
"Dread came a visiting" the islanders still say
after seeing death dancing that hurricane day.
He steered on to Florida, a killer Cat three
and slammed the panhandle refreshed from the sea.
Bridges and buildings fell to his winds
houses were shredded to toothpicks and tin.
Avast me buckos he be mean to the end
he circle around and made landfall again.

The last cane that summer gave me this twitch
hurricane Jeanne was a stone hearted witch.
When she be at sea little more than a squall
she killed thousands in Haiti, she flooded them all.
A soul thirsty wench she wasn't done yet
she did something so rare it's still hard to forget
dumbfound I be as she approached from the sea
took the same path as Frances, landfall a Cat three.
Her winds banshee shrieking even worse that before
like devil children screaming at the front of my door
torturing groaning as well from my roof overhead
if it blew away I feared ending up dead.

The shrieking night faded to an exhausted sunrise
hid behind swift moving grey and charred skies.
The roads were impassable with uprooted trees
All that were standing, stripped bare of their leaves.
But it wasn't over, the days after be cursed
a steamy quagmire that kept getting worse.
Buildings were gutted and buried in sand
Mold filled the rest the hurricane let stand.
From gale force winds to a sweltering mire
I be out of the frying pan and into the fire.
The water polluted, no food, fuel or power
I sweated and suffered, the minutes like hours.
Outdoors I be living half-baked by the sun.
Sunstroke and addled and drinking the rum.
So pay for the tale with a shot and a brew
'Tisn't believable, but I swear it be true.

**(Arr! 'Twas aft that cane season
I began talking pirate!)**

Hurricane Wilma

I'm living third world again
left where Wilma had been
it didn't take long
with the power grid gone
to devolve from computer to pen.

My house, like a castle of old
is smelling of mildew and mold
hand washing my clothes
cold showers I loathe
dump water to flush my commode.

Living like the ancestors did
Before T.V., cell phones and grid
no gas for my ride
my T.I.V.O. has died
my bedtime the same as a kids.

Living from hand to my mouth
for the civilized world's gone south
peanut butter on hand
plus all foods in a can
whatever my stomach allowth.

Oh joy! The power came on!
My A.C. sings its sweet song!
I pop a cold beer
I'm no pioneer
The modern world is where I belong!

A Florida Window

The shrieking, howling, hurricane night
got my last nerve when it blew out the lights.
The froggies outside didn't feel that way
they seemed kind of happy that hurricane day.
Croaking and beeping their amphibian tune
Like they actually enjoyed an evening typhoon.
Singing frog love songs in the winds of a cane
choral accompaniment to thunder and rain.
I found out later, that hurricane night
was exactly what made their passions ignite!
Horny frogs don't pay the hurricane no mind
it just made them dance a nice sexual wine.
While I suffered between what if and why

the frogs partied under the hurricane sky.

In the calm after, the power grid gone
Florida returned to its everglades dawn.
I sat by my window in the motionless air
suffering and sweating and stuck to my chair.
I look out in the night while praying for wind
at the tree shredded swamp-scape the gale brought in.
Silhouette and shadow from a bright pearl moon
lit up dead condos at full lunar noon.
The crickets chirp lazy, just above catatonic
languid percussion for the swamp philharmonic.
The insect musicians out there in the night
played swamp chamber music in the pale moonlight.
Florida don't pay suffering humans no mind
it just does what it does from the beginning of time.

Life's rhythm slows when modern's undone
choreographed by the rays of an über-hot sun.
For it is the maestro pulling life's strings
while we mortals below hid from its sting.
This mammal escaped the hot noon sun's rays
in my dead condo in a pre-heat stroke daze.
I looked out the window feeling kind of mid-rare
surprised to see dragonflies mate in midair!
My window and I became really good friends
as I sat and I hoped for an electrical mend.
After four sweaty nights, each one a week long
a human squeal rose up! The power came on!
We turned on the A.C., shut windows and blinds
and got back to living our pre-hurricane lives.

It took weeks to remove all the siding and tin
that was turned into junk by the hurricane wind
and months to replace all the lights that were down
the ones hardly noticed when driving around.
Florida kept on with its natural routine
it sucked up the water and turned everything green.
Shrubs once domestic, decided to go wild.
My drainage pond hadn't seen drained in a while.
It wove lush grasses among pools smooth as glass
my own personal patch of the river of grass.
The pools they were teeming with froggies brand new
and Egrets were wading eating tadpole ragout.
Hurricanes leave humans all twisted and tied
but old Florida it seems, pays them no mind.

My Favorite Window

A favorite window that I know
lives up among green pines and snow.
It gazes over a mirror lake
and cabin roofs of grayed wood shake.
Picture window, on roof top high
my transparent tapestry of earth and sky.

Early mornings on most days
the window woke me in an azure way.
Though sleepy eyes I'd take a peek
before I drifted back to sleep
at a night sky waning in denim blue
the distant mountains a darker hue.
Faint amber accents hinted day
behind the peaks a dawn away.

In an hour's instant I'm seduced to rise
by sunlight dancing upon my eyes
coaxing me from my supine state
with a sunrise if I'd wake.
Warm light dancing upon my face
releases me from sleeps embrace
rising I enjoyed the view
a sunrise window framed with dew.

A dawn voyeur, I'm mesmerized
by the art before my eyes.
Blue clouds near, still clad in night
trimmed in burgundy from the sun's first light.
Others near that dawning day
bloom to coral from the new sun's rays.
Lysergic colors, a daybreak dream
just for me or so it seemed.

Remembrances in my mind's eye
of that window's take on evening sky.
Like waking on a thunder night
to lightning clouds exploding white.
Ghost peaks flicker and fade below
from a lake reflected electric show.
Or the moon on an autumn's eve
above the lake's infinity.
Above and below a star filled sky
with a harvest moon just ridge top high.

My favorite image of them all
was on the day of a fresh snowfall.
the lake was glass, the landscape white
the sky blue brilliant, not a cloud in sight.
When I woke from a nap that day
my window pictured a bird of prey!
Framed on limb from recent flight
grey, eyes gleaming, breast snow white.
His breathing fogged the icy air
and through the window AT ME he stared.
I guess I was too big to eat
for off he flew in one wings beat.

Memories change as I age in years
some turn foggy, some disappear
but that window inside my mind
has remained unchanged thru all that time.
Somewhere near a mountain lodge
lives a window above garage.
I fondly hope it's up there still
giving up those wakeup thrills.

My Fathers Window

In the home where I grew up
to young adult from just a pup
lived a window, a stately pane
befitting my father's local fame.
He was town doctor back in a day
when house calls were the physicians way.
I didn't appreciate it then
children don't ponder what's always been
but as I've journeyed and aged in years
I've come to value what dad held dear.

It resided in his Tudor home
the kind a doctor would call his own.
In the dining room, it set the scene
It gleamed like crystal and had no seams.
Six by ten and a half inch thick
over a ledge where we kids would sit.
It framed the yard pastorally
the lush green lawn and walnut trees
a corner orchard with plums and pears
a row of currents and room to spare.
It held mom's roses and garden too
what can I say, it was quite a view!

When I muse nostalgically
my mind's eye takes me magically
through that window back to a time
when living had a slower rhyme.
Back when tulips bloomed in the spring
and robins came from southern wing.
When stars and fireflies provided light
for kid's lawn camping on summer nights.
Autumn's bon fires burned fallen leaves
and popcorn balls graced hallows' eve.
The toboggan winters of long ago
left children laughing and caked in snow.
Back when just a window pane
could keep a child entertained.

Chapter 6

Leftovers
Love, luck and laments

The Jelly Bean Tree

Once upon a road I go
I planted jelly beans in hopes they'd grow.
My friends they all made fun of me
What a silly idea! A jelly bean tree?
They laughed so hard and teased so bad
I quickly forgot the dream I had.

The years passed by for them and me
our merry band of worker bees
life takes its toll as the years roll by
young hope fades, young dreams die.
In that mood I walked the wood
on a road forgotten, there it stood!

It rose before my astounded eyes
reaching up to touch the sky!
There it grew splendiferously
my long lost dream, the jelly bean tree!
Nestled among its bright green leaves
were rainbow clusters of jelly beans!

All around it, young trees grew
full of beans plump with dew.
I gorged myself and felt so good
I started dancing in that wood.
Back in town I bought the land
and now I'm called the jellybean man.

I own a shop in our little town
selling beans to all around.
The merry band still visits me
eating jelly beans wistfully
and on the days they pass me by
I think, if not for my dream
there go I.

A Chefs Christmas

Walking dog on Christmas Day
mood and morning dark and grey.
A marinade of morning fog
dampened both me and dog
height of season, no day off
old bones felt what youth had scoffed.
Holidays had become a pill
for an old school Chef way past the thrill.

A commotion in an upstairs flat
euthanized my inner chat.
A slamming door and running feet
got me going down on the street!
I heard a child's voice exclaim
"Daddy, Daddy! LOOK HE CAME!"
I feared the worst, what could it be?
(the effect of way too much T.V.)

And then I heard the Daddy say
"I thought...last night...I heard a sleigh!"
Running feet! ..."Daddy SEE!
Look! Look! Look! at the TREEEEE!"
A happy little girl's delight.
Presents appearing overnight.
Smiling parents entertained
by a child convinced that Santa came.

That took my mood from gloom to a smile
but what happened next was really wild!
Up on the roof! It couldn't be!
Old Saint Nick was grinning at me!
The grand old elf up high on his sleigh
looking tired but happy at the end of his day.
He said "Hey Rudolf get us up out of here
but not before filling me with holiday cheer.

Yes, my blues turned to jolly and that's how I stayed
cooking the feast on that fine Christmas day.
The buffet was fantastic, my best one in years
inspired by Santa and eight tiny reindeer.
I realized then that Santa and me
had something in common professionally.
The old elf said so in his holiday way
"Merry Christmas old Chef we both work today!"

Unlikely Angel

Unlikely angel in my life
fate or happenstance?
Appearing to me after
I'd given up romance.
Like a breath upon my heart
I felt the warmth again.
From aging weekly everyday
to a lover on the mend.
Love divine, heaven sent
that's the way it seems
liberated from despair
I dream romantic dreams!

Mona Lisa

There is a place in my heart
where she lives
I don't know why, it just is.
Unknown to me the moment when
she turned to loved one from a friend.
Beyond the stars did it start
between infinity and my heart?
In between was and now
when a feeling change to vow?
I don't know all that above
I just know it's her I love
grateful that she's in my life
my pretty goddess, my dear wife.

Reflection

Something's missing in my eyes
that I used to see.
In its place a cold dark stare
looking back at me.
I wish for a time so long ago
when my eyes were bright
before lost dreams and love betrayed
removed their inner light.

Green Bug

My love she drove a green bug
She thought it best we part
All that's left, are Volkswagens
TORMENTING MY FRIGGING HEART!!

Island Woman

Conch shells, floral smells
singing everyday
eyes gleam, Island queen
beauty everyway.
Her grace, faith base
in a quiet way
Ginger tea and Cerasee
musically reggae.
Her mind, island time
calms my blues away.
I Confess, I'm blessed
with her island ways.

Regrets

Remember the day your dreams slipped away
when your future was less than your past?
The how, when and why of youth slipping by
Unnoticed as life slowly past?
When came the time when life lost its rhyme
and the role of sweet youth was re-cast?
The when, where and what of a middle aged rut
when I changed to cautious from brash?
As I sit here and write of my years taking flight
how what was once slow became fast.
I research alibis on the how, where and whys
of a future that's slipped from my grasp.

Velvet Knife

Please I beg, you my dear wife
have mercy with your velvet knife
You wield it matter-of-factly,
so cool, so calm, so exactly
creative, cold, staccato blows,
from a lover who's come to know
my faults and failings
changing me from lover to liability.
I real from a thousand blows
struck by a stranger I used to know
clueless to the moment we,
changed from "couple" into a me.
lost and hollow, deaf in a fog
handsome prince turned back to frog.

Alone is.....

A dark forest
> **i never leave.**

A whisper
> **strained to hear.**

A grey sky
> **on a cold day.**

A stagnant soul filled
> **with rotting happiness.**

Alone
> **is my heart**

My chest
> **aches with it.**

My eyes
> **tear from it.**

It is what I embrace.
> **It is what I fear.**

Life is
> **echo and canyon**

I am

> a

> l

> o

> n

> e.....

**An old island saying
"Alone is better than bad company"
after the great love of my life fell
apart I see the wisdom in that phrase.**

Poems Dancing

I don't write poems they write me
attention deficit epiphanies.
Verbal ditties paired in rhyme
dancing about my porous mind.
I love it when they're play up there
like butterflies without a care.
I dearly hope they'll always stay
And continue with their rhyming play.
They're a favorite gift of mine.
These rhyming rhythms in my mind.

The night before election 2004

T' was the night before election and all through da house
the traitor Dems were thinking G.W.'s a louse.
The Pubies they were all tucked in their beds
dreaming of ways to turn blue states to red!
But hark on the roof what's the sound that I hear?
It's ol' President Clinton, full of good cheer!
"Don't worry my friends, I feel your pain
y'all got to remember it is all just a game.
The election will tie and the congress will too
you know that bunch can't decide anything new.
The Supreme Court will deadlock, cause Rehnquist is ill
and then no one is left to decide on the hill.
The lawyers will lawyer and the pundits will cry
but you don't have to worry and I'm telling you why.
"After W. and Kerry are too tired to fight
as well as all those on the left and the right
the voters will wish for a return to the past
and I will be President, once again, at long last!"

Flicker

Feeling the child again I sit
helpless participant.
The hospital room
eerie at night
Pop's ghostly white
as a faulty hall light
flickers.

Post-op drugged
the one I feared
with whom I fought
and in the clarity of crisis
who I loved
as a child loves
struggles in the night.
I watch him
I feel him
flicker.

He's somewhe between
awake and sleeping
between pain and
healing laying there
helpless and apart
lost in the dark
a twitch, a groan,
a whisper
a flicker.

The holidays are here
the grandkids are down
his favorite thing lost
in a hospital room's twilight.
Between life and death.
Between hope and fear.
Helplessly I sit
his child waiting
and hoping
for more
than a
flicker.

Poor Penny
(a poem for lotto scratch off addicts like me)

Poor penny, poor penny, do your lotto thing
work your copper magic for I need prospering!
I always pick the poorest penny dwelling in my jar
and use it for my scratch offs, my lotto scimitar.
I pick an ugly penny, tarnished, dull and worn
it just has to be a talisman, being humble born.
So pretty please, poor penny, do your magic thing
help me scratch this scratch off so I can get some bling!

**(Guaranteed to bring you as much luck
as an E mail chain letter.)**

Old Folks Moan

What used to be crazy, isn't
People walk, muttering to themselves
Then I see their "blue tooth"
Males with purses, insisting they're not
Laptop? I got a bridge to sell you!
What do you mean? What do I mean!
Furtive glances, defensive stances
My rumpled persona sitting and starring
enhances the pace of the mall walkers passing by
a muttering, blue toothless,
old man...

The Chef's Special
(adultish)

A German Cheffie (withheld name)
had a dish of local fame
it wasn't veal, it wasn't game
yet quite tasty all the same.
It was "sasiccia" as the Italians say
but prepared the German way!

All the waitresses scream and shout
Cheffie whip your knockwurst out!
It's so plump and red and stout
it's something we all talk about!
But we all say without a doubt
why does it smell like sauerkraut?

An American waitress cute and fine
talked of recipes all the time
I have one Chef, it's so divine
show me yours, I'll show you mine.
Hers of course, warm apple pie
Cheffie wanted it, we all know why.

The American girl screams and shouts
your Knockwurst is without a doubt
plump and red and big and stout
I'm happy to watch you whip it out!
But what do the girls all talk about?
What the heck is sauerkraut?

Well our Cheffie, that very day
prepared his Knockwurst veloute.
Once she smelled it, she said no way
but he made her eat it anyway!
Of course he gave her dish a try
but all guys like warm apple pie!

All the waitresses scream and shout
you Cheffies get your Knockwursts out!
They're so plump and red and stout
we love to watch you whip them out!
We like them now, we had some doubt
we even like the sauerkraut!

Coexist

Made in the USA
Lexington, KY
02 April 2019